BLACK LEGACY PRESS™
WWW.BLACKLEGACYPRESS.ORG

The Agricultural and Forest Products of British West Africa
By
Gerald C. Dudgeon

Copyright © 2024 by BLACKLEGACYPRESS.ORG
All rights reserved. No part of this publication may be reproduced or transmitted in any form or by any means electronic or mechanical, including information storage and retrieval systems without permission in writing from the publisher, except for student research using the appropriate citations.

ISBN: 978-1-63652-414-6

THE AGRICULTURAL AND FOREST PRODUCTS OF BRITISH WEST AFRICA

GERALD C. DUDGEON

CONTENTS

PREFACE TO THE SECOND EDITION 1

PREFACE TO THE FIRST EDITION 4

THE GAMBIA 6

SIERRA LEONE 30

THE GOLD COAST, ASHANTI AND THE
NORTHERN TERRITORIES 70

NIGERIA-SOUTHERN PROVINCES 142

NIGERIA-NORTHERN PROVINCES 184

PREFACE TO THE SECOND EDITION

SINCE the first edition of this book appeared, British West Africa has experienced a serious set-back in its development through the occurrence of the Great European War. From that war, however, many lessons will have been learnt, which will, it is hoped, make the course of progress in the future more sure and perhaps more rapid.

The cultivation of cotton has now been shown to be successful and profitable in Nigeria. In the Northern Provinces great progress has been made in perfecting a cotton originally grown from "American Upland" seed, whilst the Southern Provinces have produced increasing quantities of an improved native cotton of the type of "Middling American." The future of cotton production in Nigeria is now assured, and its further development chiefly depends on effective action being taken on commercial lines.

The products of the oil palm and especially palm kernels have been in increased demand for edible purposes, the war having led to a far greater use of margarine and similar materials. The perfection of processes for the better extraction of palm oil from the fruits which had nearly reached success at the outbreak of war now awaits completion, when a large additional source of edible oil will be available. In the meantime the trial cultivation of this palm in other countries has been attended with remarkable success, the growth of the palm in plantations having been entirely satisfactory and furnished yields of oil which exceed those given by the wild palm in West Africa. The Dutch East Indies, where large plantations have been made, and also British Malaya, where similar enterprise has been shown, may before long be formidable rivals to West Africa in the production of palm kernels and palm oil. The neglect in West Africa of the wild trees, the imperfect methods followed in extracting the palm oil, and the large number of palms unutilised are questions which now need renewed attention, and in fact the entire subject of the development of the palm-oil industry in West Africa demands the most serious study in all its aspects if the industry is not to be supplanted by the enterprise of other countries.

In this and other directions where the continuous acquisition of new knowledge is requisite, it is satisfactory to learn that the staffs of the Agricultural Departments in West Africa are to be extended and better remunerated. In addition to this step, and perhaps equally important, will be the increased interest and activity of those merchants and manufacturers who utilise the raw materials of the country, and to whom the commercial development of West Africa has hitherto owed so much.

There are many other subjects which, it will be seen from the new edition of this book, have come to the front since the first edition appeared, and now need increased attention.

The only rubber tree which has survived as a producer in the years of strenuous competition is *Hevea brasiliensis*, from which Para rubber is obtained. Successful plantations of this tree have been established both in the Southern Provinces of Nigeria and in the Gold Coast, and from the former commercial rubber is now being produced of quality equal to that of the rubber plantations of the East.

The Gold Coast has become the chief cocoa producer of the world, but it is clear that unremitting care and attention in connection with the cultivation and the preparation of cocoa in that country will be necessary if that supremacy is to be maintained.

In connection with the production of fibres, cinchona bark, cinnamon, tobacco, and many other materials, there are promising possibilities in various parts of West Africa, including those new territories for which, as a result of the war, Great Britain is now responsible. Above all, there is the dominant problem of the growth of foodstuffs sufficient to maintain the native populations of these countries.

Mr. Dudgeon, within the limits imposed in the production of a revised but not greatly enlarged edition, has successfully brought this Handbook up-to-date, and it is hoped that it will continue to serve as a standard guide to all those who require general information respecting the agricultural and forest products of West Africa.

WYNDHAM R. DUNSTAN.

Imperial Institute,
March 1921.

PREFACE TO THE FIRST EDITION

THE present series of Handbooks is intended to present a general account of the principal commercial resources of the tropics, and has been written with special reference to the resources of British West Africa. These Handbooks will furnish a description of the occurrence, cultivation and uses of those tropical materials, such as cotton and other fibres, cocoa, rubber, oil-seeds, tobacco, etc., which are of importance to the producer in the tropics, as well as to the manufacturer and consumer in Europe.

Without attempting to include all the detailed information of a systematic treatise on each of the subjects included, it is believed that these Volumes will contain much information which will be of value to the tropical agriculturist as well as to the merchant and manufacturer. They will also be of importance to Government Officials in tropical Colonies where the advancement of the Country and the welfare of its inhabitants depend so largely on the development of natural resources. In recent years those candidates who are selected for administrative appointments under the Colonial Office in British West Africa are required to pass through a short course of instruction in tropical cultivation and products, which is now arranged at the Imperial Institute. For these prospective officials the present series of Handbooks will be helpful in the study of a large and generally unfamiliar subject. Similarly it is believed that the series will provide a valuable aid to the teaching of commercial geography. It is hoped also that the Handbooks will not be without interest for the student of Imperial and national problems.

The increase in the productivity of the tropics, and especially of the tropical regions within the British Empire, is important, not only for the natives of those countries, and others who are actually engaged in tropical enterprise, but for the merchant and manufacturer at home. The preparation for general use of cotton and other fibres, of tea, coffee and cocoa, of oils, of tobacco, and of numerous other products exported from the tropics, provides the means of employment and livelihood for a very large proportion of the working population of this country, whilst every one at home is interested in securing an adequate supply at a moderate cost of these necessaries and luxuries of life.

The subjects of these Handbooks, treated as they will be, as far as possible, in non-technical language, should therefore appeal to a large class of readers.

The present Handbook deals with the Agricultural and Forest Products of British West Africa and serves as an introduction to this series. Mr. Dudgeon, who until lately was Inspector of Agriculture in the West African Colonies and Protectorates, writes with an unrivalled knowledge of his subject, and gives a comprehensive account of the vegetable products of that country, which will afford to the general reader some idea of the enormous possibilities of this British territory now in the process of rapid commercial development.

WYNDHAM R. DUNSTAN.

Imperial Institute, S.W.
March 1911.

THE GAMBIA

INTRODUCTORY REMARKS. Geographical Position.—The Gambia Colony and Protectorate consists of a narrow tract of country following the winding course of the river from which it takes its name, for a distance of about 250 miles, and extending approximately four miles from the river on both banks.

The whole country lies between 12° 10' and 13° 15' north latitude and 13° 50' and 16° 40' west longitude. It is the most northerly of the British West African possessions.

Area and Population.—The extent of territory is said to be 3,619 square miles, much of which consists of low-lying land intersected by creeks and rivers, which under tidal influence are often densely afforested with mangroves.

According to the census of 1911 the Colony and Protectorate had populations of 7,700 and 138,401 respectively, totalling 146,101. The total of 90,404 given in the previous census is now admitted to have been below the actual amount. A large migratory farming community exists, coming annually from the adjoining countries, for the purpose of raising groundnut crops. This in 1911 numbered 3,367. Many of these immigrants are reported to have remained and established themselves permanently under the British flag.

Tribes.—The principal tribes inhabiting the Gambia are the Mandingoes, Foulahs, Joloffs, and Jolahs. The first-named are the most numerous, and are, generally speaking, Mohammedans, although there are many "Sonninkis" or spirit drinkers among them. The Foulahs are identical with the Fulanis of the Gold Coast and Northern Nigeria, and are frequently fair-skinned without negroid features. They are said to be strictly Mohammedan, and to have originated from the country near the source of the Senegal river. The Joloffs occupy the northern bank of the Gambia river, and extend well into Senegal. The Jolahs inhabit the province of Fogni, and spread into the confines of French territory towards the Casamance river. They are a curious race, given to living in small family villages, and are said to be vindictive. They are of a lower type than the three other tribes mentioned, and are jealous of their rights.

Political Divisions.—The Protectorate is divided into five districts, each under the control of a Travelling Commissioner. These districts are named in accordance with their positions: North Bank, South Bank, M'Carthy Island, Kommbo and Fogni, and Upper River.

Natural Conditions.—The climatic conditions of the country are favourable to the breeding of cattle and horses, although in the vicinity of the river and creeks two species of tsetse fly are common. By carefully preventing animals from straying into these infested tracts the spread of fly-borne disease is held in check, and cases are comparatively rare.

During the dry season, which often occupies seven months in the year, from November to May, the highest maximum and the lowest minimum temperatures are recorded; the range being from 41° (lowest minimum, March 1909) to 105° (highest maximum, March 1909 and April 1911). The rainfall, of which official records are kept at Bathurst, varies considerably, as the following extract will serve to show:

1901	45·31	inches	1910	44·00	inches
1902	29·42	,,	1911	28·14	,,
1903	57·13	,,	1912	33·99	,,
1904	38·02	,,	1913	23·68	,,
1905	66·07	,,	1914	48·91	,,
1906	64·36	,,	1915	47·64	,,
1907	34·00	,,	1916	38·02	,,
1908	43·54	,,	1917	37·68	,,
1909	56·59	,,	1918	54·03	,,

Soil.—The soil generally is of a light sandy nature, becoming stiffer as the undulating regions of the upper river are approached. The low countries are subject to flood in the rainy season, and are only favourable for rice cultivation.

JOLAH WITH NATIVE HAND-PLOUGH, BULLELAI, FOGNI.
FIG. 1

CANARY ISLAND PLOUGH, AGRICULTURAL SCHOOL, ABUKO.
Fig. 2

RUBBER TREE (*FICUS VOGELII*) AT BATHURST.
Fig. 3

Chief Crops.—The country is rather sparsely populated, but, on the whole, the people are fair cultivators and prepare their lands in a careful manner. Practically the only crop grown for export is the groundnut, monkey-nut, or earth-pea (*Arachis hypogæa*), which forms by far the most important article of cultivation. Alternating this with the staple food-crops of the country, namely, guinea-corn, maize, millet, and cassava, a fairly useful form of rotation is obtained.

Implements.—Cultivation among the Mandingoes and Joloffs is performed by means of a large wooden-bladed, iron-shod hoe, with which the loose earth ridges are thrown up. A small iron hoe is used for keeping down weeds and clearing. In the Jolah country a handplough is employed, consisting of a flat blade attached to a pole, and pushed in front of the operator, so as to throw up a shallow ridge. This is shown in the picture which represents a native with the implement at Bullelai (Fig. 1).

Ploughing.—Cattle are plentiful, even to the extent of there being an insufficiency of fodder for them in the dry season in some localities. They are chiefly kept for the purpose of displaying the wealth of their owners, and are not employed for any kind of farm work. Notwithstanding the shortage of manual labour and the successful demonstrations made by the Government, through the agency of the Roman Catholic Fathers at the Abuko Agricultural School, to prove the value of substituting animal draught for manual labour in tilling the land, the prejudice on the part of the natives against the use of their cattle for ploughing or cartage has not been overcome. A photograph is given showing a native with a Canary Island plough drawn by locally-trained bullocks (Fig. 2). Owing to the failure attending the efforts to introduce ploughing and cattle breeding at Abuko, where, for the latter purpose, some Ayrshire bulls were provided, the Govermnent withdrew the provisional subsidy in 1911.

Land Tenure.—Land ownership is hereditary and descends from father to son among the Mandingoes and Joloffs. No fees are paid or presents given to chiefs when a transfer is made. Europeans can rent land from Government in cases where it is not held or claimed by a native. Grants are apparently issued for various periods, but freehold rights are not given.

The rules regarding the itinerant, so-called "strange farmers," who annually visit the country to plant groundnuts, vary to some extent in different parts of the Protectorate. Where hereditary ruling chiefs exist, a tax of 4*s*. per head is paid to them. In other places, half of this tax goes to Government, one-quarter to the chief, and one-quarter to the farmer's landlord. The landowner generally gives the groundnut seed and food as well as a piece of land to be cultivated. In payment for the seed and food, it is a rule to give one-tenth of the crop. During the time the strange farmer is in occupation he is expected to give one or two days' work each week on the landowner's own farm.

Labour.—There is no fixed rate paid by the Government for labour. All the work on a farm is done by the owner and his own boys, but occasionally others come in to assist from the neighbouring farms, but no payment is made—only a present of kolas being usually given.

Agricultural Schools.—An agricultural school, previously referred to, was started at Abuko, near Lammin, under the Roman Catholic Fathers there, and a subsidy was granted by the Government especially for the purpose of educating the sons of large cultivators and chiefs in the use of ploughs and other labour-saving implements. A stipulation was made that the work should be inspected by a Government officer from time to time.

In spite of this a fear was expressed at the outset that the attendance at these schools would be disappointing, in view of the fact that Mohammedan chiefs would be restrained by their mallams from sending their children where there might be a risk of their religious conversion. Although it had been specially laid down that no religious teaching would be insisted upon, the fear proved justified and the school never became a success, the attendance being only of a few aliens. Since the closing of this school no renewal of agricultural instruction seems to have been made.

Chief Exports.—The following table gives the average amounts and values of the chief exports for 1900-10, and the individual figures for the remaining years to 1918.

Year	Groundnuts tons and value	Rubber lbs. and value	Beeswax lbs. and value	Palm Kernels tons and value
1900-10 Av.	39,000 tons £250,000	46,000 lbs. £3,500	45,500 lbs. £2,000	255 tons £2,260
1911	47,931 tons £437,472	10,733 lbs. £836	33,871 lbs. £1,514	443 tons £4,758
1912	64,169 tons £502,069	4,335 lbs. £409	30,830 lbs. £1,164	445 tons £6,518
1913	67,404 tons £622,098	12,995 lbs. £1,027	31,518 lbs. £990	546 tons £9,026
1914	66,885 tons £650,461	3,548 lbs. £102	15,513 lbs. £473	495 tons £7,815
1915	96,152 tons £400,435	1,171 lbs. £31	9,563 lbs. £311	326 tons £5,457
1916	46,366 tons £506,098	355 lbs. £23	6,950 lbs. £104	669 tons £14,671
1917	74,300 tons £869,790	1,753 lbs. £187	3,962 lbs. £247	532 tons £7,994
1918	56,489 tons £800,319	564 lbs. £40	8,626 lbs. £501	644 tons £9,800

Note.—Cotton exports were 59,828 lbs. and 2,572 lbs. in 1904 and 1905 respectively. None has been exported since.

GROUNDNUTS.—This commodity is by far the most important exported product, and is alone subject to a duty levied by the Administration.

Uses.—The undecorticated nuts are shipped, chiefly, to the

French ports and to Hamburg, for the expression of an oil of excellent quality, of which they yield on an average about 30 per cent., estimated on the weight of the raw material. This is equivalent to about 44 per cent. of the weight of the extracted kernels.

The mode of extraction in general employment in France is to grind the kernels into a fine meal, from which the first quality of oil is extracted by cold expression, yielding about 18 per cent. The meal is then moistened with cold water, and at the second expression 6 per cent. more is obtained. Both of these oils are useful for alimentary purposes. A third expression is made from the residue treated with hot water, and gives a further 6 per cent., which is chiefly employed for lighting purposes, lubricating and soap-making. The fine oils are substituted for, or mixed with, the olive-oils of commerce for salad oils, and enter into the manufacture of oleo-margarine. After these expressions of oil have been made, the meal is pressed into cakes and used for cattle-food and manurial purposes.

Classification and Description of the Groundnut Plant.— The groundnut belongs to the Sub-Order *Papilionaceæ*, of the Order *Leguminosæ*, and is termed *Arachis hypogæa*, Linn.

The plant cultivated in Senegal and the Gambia grows in a spreading form, with branches of from 12 to 18 inches in length, and possesses oval leaflets given off in double pairs. A large number of conspicuous yellow flowers appear from the upper leaf axils, but are not capable of fertilisation. Those springing from the lower leaf axils nearest the ground are small and generally hidden, but produce fruitful pods. After fertilisation the stems of these flowers become elongated, and are directed downwards, forcing the ovary into the ground, in which it commences to swell to the mature size, frequently penetrating to a depth of two inches beneath the surface.

The fruit is a pale straw-coloured, irregularly-cylindrical pod, with the surface of the shell pitted and longitudinally ribbed. In the Gambian variety, which is identical with the common Senegalese kind, there are usually two kernels in each pod, but three or one are also found.

The plant is of doubtful origin, but it is generally supposed that it may have been introduced into Africa from Brazil (where the genus *Arachis* is well represented) nearly four centuries ago, by the Portuguese slave-traders.

About 1840 groundnuts began to attract the attention of European manufacturers, on account of the value of the oil obtained from them, and, in common with the Senegalese, the Gambian natives were induced to undertake cultivation upon a large scale.

The nuts grown in the Gambia and in Saloum, in the French territory adjoining on the north, are classed as of second quality; those from Cayor and Rufisque holding the first, and those from the Casamance and Portuguese Guinea the third, places.

The seeds are sown upon ridges with flattened tops, and the crop occupies the ground for about four months—July to October—corresponding to the period of heavy rainfall in the country. When the branches commence to wither, the whole plant is carefully pulled up, so that the pods, which are then mature, remain attached. The plants are then stacked in the fields, and are often covered over with the leaves of the fan-palm. The green parts dry into a hay, which, when the pods have been beaten out, is used as horse-fodder. The advent of rain after stacking often does great damage to the crop, but the occurrence is so rare that it has been found difficult to induce the native to take common precautions against it. During the last two years, however, the Government have taken steps to enforce a regulation with regard to this, and in consequence drains are now generally cut around the stacks, and coverings of palm-leaves are left on until the nuts are ready to be beaten out.

In the Jolah country raised platforms are constructed for stacking this crop as well as others. After the nuts have been beaten out from the dried plants, they are winnowed by allowing them to fall from a slight elevation in a gentle breeze.

A good crop of nuts in the Gambia is estimated at about 44 bushels per acre, equivalent to over half a ton, but larger yields are frequently obtained. The Government standard bushel is used throughout the country, and may contain from 25 to 31 lbs. of undecorticated nuts.

Experiments have been made from time to time, to establish a three-kernel nut instead of the two-kernel one, but the results obtained have not shown that any advantage could be gained in this way. Other varieties of nuts have been introduced and cultivated, but no extensive planting of new kinds has yet been found worth adoption.

The plant seldom suffers from severe attacks of disease, although a white fungus was prevalent in some localities in 1906. This affection was termed "tio jarankaro" by the Mandingoes. In the succeeding year it completely disappeared, and has not been reported to have occurred since. The extermination of this disease was doubtless in a large measure due to the careful way in which the selection and distribution of seed had been carried out. For several years the Government has been accustomed to purchase a certain quantity of the best nuts each season, and to distribute these at sowing time to the cultivators, on credit. Without this precaution, in a season when the prices for nuts were high, the thriftless native would be induced to sell every nut, reserving nothing for sowing the next year. The system adopted is greatly appreciated by the cultivators and merchants alike, and has without doubt contributed largely to the prosperity of the country. Seed is not only interchanged, in this manner, with advantage between different districts, but fresh seed is sometimes also provided from Senegal.

The immigrant or "strange farmers" are generally welcomed by the land-owners, who usually manage to lease them the fields which require the most cleaning. After the immigrant farmer has reaped his groundnut crop, the field is left in a good state of tilth for the owner to sow his guinea corn.

The occurrence of ruinous competition among merchants at Bathurst induced them to form a "combine" to regulate the buying price of nuts; the purchases being pooled and then divided according to a fixed scale. A recent attempt to divert Gambian nuts to Senegal ports for shipment, by the levy of an import tax at Marseilles, was opposed by the French and British merchants alike, and the fear that the produce might only be diverted to another destination led to its abandonment. For further information regarding the cultivation, varieties and uses of groundnuts, see *Bulletin of the Imperial Institute*, vol. viii. (1910), pp. 153-72.

RUBBER.—A good quality of rubber is produced in the Jolah country, in particular, from *Landolphia Heudelotii*, an apocynaceous vine, which grows commonly in the grass lands of Fogni.

The vine is tapped by women, who, after digging a hole near

the root of the plant, make a number of transverse cuts upon the root-stem. The latex flows rapidly from such cuts, and is coagulated by throwing salt water on the wound. The scrap rubber which forms is collected the following day, and the pieces are attached to one another, forming an open sponge-like ball of a pinkish-white colour. Sand is often present in these balls owing to the fallen latex being added to the rest.

RUBBER VINE (*LANDOLPHIA HEUDELOTII*) AT KOTOO.
Fig. 4

CEARA RUBBER TREE (*MANIHOT GLAZIOVII*) AT BAKAU.
Fig. 5

RUBBER TREE (*CASTILLOA ELASTICA*) AT KOTOO.
FIG. 6

In addition to the inhabitants themselves collecting rubber, natives belonging to a tribe from Portuguese Guinea, called "Manjagos," travel through the country for the purpose; the rubber which they obtain being sold in the French Colony to the south of the Gambia. The "Manjagos" are said to make a semicircular cut upon the thick vine-stems just above the ground, to induce the better flow of latex. This, they maintain, is not a destructive method, and that, as the root stock is uninjured, the plant continues to yield latex for a long time. At one time the rubber vine must have been plentiful, but the rush for it which occurred at the beginning of the present century has had the effect of exterminating it, except in the more inaccessible places. The export has declined and is now insignificant. The plant is known to the Mandingoes as "Folio." An illustration is given showing this plant at Kotoo (Fig. 4).

Landolphia florida, Benth., is common in places similar to those where the last-mentioned vine occurs, but the latex is not used in any way to adulterate the good rubber, nor is inferior "paste" rubber made from it, as in other places in West Africa. *Ficus Vogelii*, known as "Kobbo" (Mandingo), has recently been used for extracting an inferior rubber, which has been shipped in small quantities. This tree is found growing in Bathurst as well as in many of the large towns, where it often attains a large size, and affords an excellent shade for native markets, etc. A view of a tree in Bathurst is shown (Fig. 3). Information regarding the composition and value of the rubber of *Ficus Vogelii* is given in the *Bulletin of the Imperial Institute*, vol. vii. (1909), p. 260.

Some of the South American species of rubber trees have been planted at different places, but for the most part the climatic conditions have proved unsuitable for their establishment. An exception to this is the Ceara rubber (*Manihot Glaziovii*), large trees of which were to be seen in Bathurst and at Bakau, but in the latter locality appear to have been cut down during recent years. It is generally acknowledged that Ceara rubber has not proved successful in plantations made in different parts of West Africa, for, although rubber of the finest quality can be easily prepared from the latex, the tree furnishes an extremely inconstant yield of latex. In the Gambia the tree reproduces readily, and, as far as can be judged, produces a latex capable of being coagulated into good rubber. As a shade tree it is recommended to be grown along public roads, and it might prove expedient in the country to make small experimental plantations, in the manner adopted in Togoland and elsewhere. By this system, tapping is continued for a few years, and whole blocks of trees are cut out as they cease to yield latex—the seedlings which have sprung up beneath these trees being permitted to take the place of the original trees. An illustration showing a Ceara rubber tree at Bakau is given (Fig. 5).

One specimen of *Castilloa elastica*, of which a photograph is given (Fig. 6), is growing in the Kotoo farm, about 12 miles from Bathurst. This tree has not, so far, proved successful in West Africa, and the example photographed is apparently in better condition than those grown in the Botanic Gardens of the Gold Coast and Southern Nigeria.

Funtumia elastica, the Lagos silk rubber tree, does not thrive in the Gambia, and the rainfall has been found to be insufficiently distributed for the cultivation of the Para rubber tree (*Hevea brasiliensis*).

The observed facts point to the conclusion that further

experimental trials of certain species of rubber trees in the Gambia should be made.

BEESWAX.—It will be observed that a large quantity of beeswax is annually exported, the quality of which is high. The native bee is a small form of *Apis mellifera*, var. *Adansonii*. It is found in a wild state forming nests in hollow trees or rock cavities. The Mandingoes collect the wild swarms and confine them in basket-hives, cylindrical in form and sometimes plastered over with mud. These are placed in high trees or in abandoned huts. The wax is sold in a crude form to the Bathurst merchants, who boil it down and strain it previous to shipment. The European market value of the cleaned wax is from £5 to £6 per cwt. A detailed description of methods for the refining of wild bees' wax for export is published in the *Bulletin of the Imperial Institute*, vol. viii. (1910), pp. 23-31.

PALM KERNELS.—The West African oil palm, *Elæis guineensis*, is found commonly in some parts, but the heads produced are small and carry small fruits, containing little oil. This oil is used locally, and the kernels from the nuts alone are shipped. The palm is chiefly valued for the production of palm wine, which is tapped from the base of the fruiting stems into funnelled gourds, hung beneath the holes. The tree is apparently never felled for the purpose, and, by limiting the amount of wine extracted, it survives for a long period.

COTTON.—The Mandingoes and Jolahs cultivate cotton for making the yarn used in their native looms, in which they weave the strips of cloth called "pagns." These strips are afterwards sewn together along their lateral edges and made into gowns.

The native cotton plant varies somewhat in appearance. In

Kommbo, a long straggling form occurs, which is retained for two seasons to produce cotton, but in the Jolah country a small annual is most frequently seen. The former is grown as a mixed crop and the latter in separate patches.

In quality, from the European spinner's point of view, the Mandingo cotton lint compares favourably with the commercial type called "middling American" as far as length of staple is concerned, although it is not so white, nor is there so much silkiness apparent. It has been rightly remarked that the native variety, if properly cultivated, would probably give a better result than would be obtained from the introduction of American seed. The Jolah cotton is short-stapled and woolly, though whiter than the Mandingo. It would be more difficult to improve this kind sufficiently to suit the European demand.

Egyptian cotton seed was tried in the Gambia about twenty years ago, and the variety was at first considered suitable; the cultivation was, however, not proceeded with, owing to local difficulties.

The obstacles which hindered the development of cotton-growing in the Gambia for export were the same as those experienced in Sierra Leone. The local demand for raw cotton precluded it from being obtained at a sufficiently low price to leave a margin of profit to exporters, and in addition to this, labour was not sufficiently abundant, nor were the natives familiar with labour-saving methods in cultivation. Attempts to establish an interest in the matter produced a fair amount of raw cotton in 1904, but since that year the exported quantity rapidly diminished and has now ceased altogether. For reports on the quality of the cotton produced in the Gambia see Professor Dunstan's *British Cotton Cultivation* (Colonial Reports—Miscellaneous Series, Cd. 3997,

1908), p. 26, and *Bull. Imp. Inst.*, 1921. Samples may be seen in the Imperial Institute Collections.

GRAIN CROPS.—No grain is exported, as owing to the work of the scanty population being so largely applied to the cultivation of groundnuts, scarcely sufficient food-stuff is grown for their own requirements. Guinea-corn (*Sorghum vulgare*), the two most important varieties of which are known as "Bassi" and "Kinto" in the Mandingo language, are commonly used for food, but during recent years, owing to the repeated annual attacks on the crop by *Aphis sorghi*, maize-growing was substituted in some parts of the country. White maize seed was obtained from Lagos, and yellow maize seed from the Canary Islands, but the grain is not appreciated to the same extent as Guinea corn. *Pennisetum typhoideum*, the large millet, of which the commonest variety is known in Mandingo as "Sannio," is alternated with Guinea corn or maize, but is often badly affected by a "smut fungus" (*Ustilago sp.*), which also attacks the "Kinto" variety of Guinea corn. A small grass is often grown in the millet fields, yielding a crop of fine seed which is made into flour for the preparation of a kind of porridge. This is termed "Findi" locally. Rice (*Oryza sativa*) is somewhat extensively grown in the swamp lands, but the success of the crop is very largely dependent on the distribution of the rainfall. Whole tracts of rice fields are destroyed in some years, owing to excessive floods, as no precautions are taken to guard against them. It is chiefly on account of the uncertainty of the grain crops, that a large quantity of rice has to be imported annually to supplement that produced in the country. These imports often amount to six or seven thousand tons.

FRUITS OF OIL PALMS, SIERRA LEONE.
Fig. 9

SWEET CASSAVA, WITH BAOBAB TREES, BAKAU.
Fig. 7

INDIGO DYERS, McCARTHY ISLAND.
FIG. 8

ROOT AND OTHER CROPS.—Sweet cassava (*Manihot palmata*) is frequently planted as a terminal crop in the crude rotation employed. This variety can be eaten without previously washing or cooking. An illustration of a cassava field is given (Fig. 7). Two or three kinds of beans are planted, though not extensively in spite of a good local demand for them. Okra (*Hibiscus esculentus*), cultivated for the edible fruit pods, indigo (*Indigofera sp.*) employed for making the local blue dye, and tobacco (*Nicotiana tabacum*), are planted near houses. A photograph is given exhibiting the different utensils required for the preparation of indigo, and cakes of the dried and fermented indigo stalks, in the form in which they are preserved, are shown suspended in the illustration (Fig. 8). The tobacco prepared is usually ground into snuff, in which form it is used for chewing as well as for smoking.

TANNING.—Goat-skins are tanned in the manner similar

to that employed by the Haussas; *Acacia arabica* pods being used in the process. The people who perform the work of preparing and working leather are termed "Korankos." Red and black inks, purchased from the European merchants, are used for staining the leather, which is inferior to that produced in Northern Nigeria.

FIBRES.—The country seems to be plentifully supplied with fibre plants in a wild state, chiefly belonging to different species of *Hibiscus*. These are of the jute class, and are used throughout the country for making native ropes. Indian jute (*Corchorus capsularis*) has been tried experimentally at Kotoo, and excellent samples were obtained, but the quantity of fibre per acre turned out to be small, and the working proved to be too expensive.

The preparation of piassava, which had been abandoned for many years, is said to have been taken up again by a British firm in 1915. The fibre is obtained from the leaf sheath of a palm (*Raphia vinifera*) which grows plentifully along the banks of the Gambia in places. For further information see *Selected Reports from the Imperial Institute*, Pt. I., Fibres, and *Bull. Imp. Inst.*, 1915.

TIMBER.—There are no trees of commercial importance, accessible for felling for export, although Gambian mahogany (*Khaya senegalensis*) and Gambian rosewood (*Pterocarpus erinaceus*) occur in many parts of the country. In some remote districts the former tree is said to attain large dimensions (*Bulletin of the Imperial Institute*, vol. viii. (1910), p. 244).

TRADE.—The following extracts from the Colonial Reports show the diversion of destination of Gambian exports which has occurred in recent years. For this purpose groundnuts are regarded as representing the whole of the trade, of which they normally constitute about 90 per cent.

Percentages of Exports from the Gambia

Destination	1911	1912	1913	1914	1915	1916	1917
Great Britain and British Possessions	6·30	9·00	6·72	9·92	39·45	53·56	79·56
France and French Possessions	84·80	76·00	59·10	79·34	48·60	36·58	20·35
Holland	3·20	9·00	6·03	—	—	4·20	—
Germany	—	3·64	24·56	6·80	—	—	—
Denmark	—	—	—	1·99	7·68	5·63	—
Spain	—	—	—	·35	4·24	—	—
Other countries	5·70	2·36	3·59	1·60	0·03	0·03	0·09
	100	100	100	100	100	100	100

From the above it will be noted that Germany began to appear in the market in 1912, and, in 1913, had taken nearly one-quarter of the output. This is probably accounted for by the rapid growth of the vegetable oil industry in Germany and the attempt on the part of Hamburg crushers to capture the Gambia trade from Marseilles. It will be seen that a proportionate decrease occurred in exports to French ports coincident with the increased shipments to German ports. The European war put Germany out of the market, and in 1914 France took nearly her normal share. In 1915 and 1916, however, Great Britain felt the lack of imported vegetable oils to such an extent that factories for their extraction sprang up in the country; thus it is seen that in 1915 Great Britain took nearly 40 per cent. against France's 48½ per cent., and in 1916, Great Britain, for the first time in the last fifty years, took a larger portion of the Gambian groundnut crop than France.

GAMBIA & SIERRA LEONE

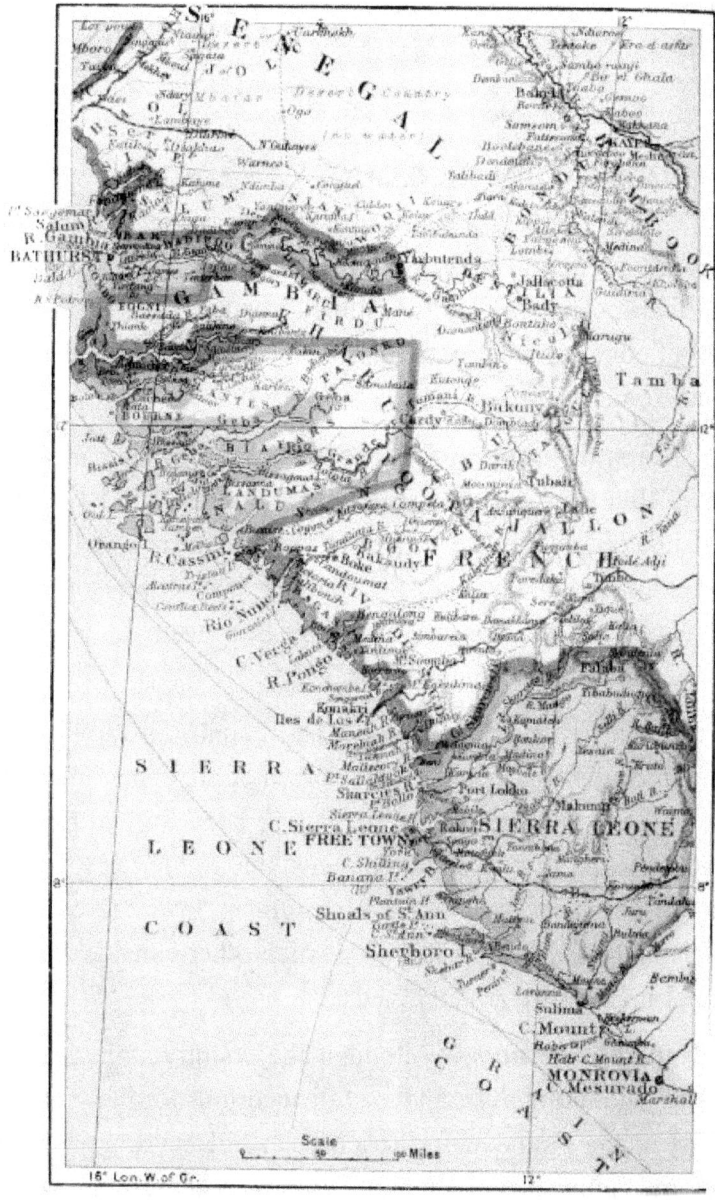

Stanford's Geogl. Estabt., London.

SIERRA LEONE

INTRODUCTORY REMARKS. Geographical Position.—The Colony and Protectorate of Sierra Leone are bounded upon the north and west by French Guinea, and upon the east by Liberia. The Colony is confined to the hill country of the Sierra Leone Peninsula and Sherbro Island; the remainder being Protectorate.

Area and Population.—The area of the country according to the Blue Book of 1911 is 31,000 sq. miles. The greater part is undulating, well watered and fairly fertile, traversed by short ranges of mountains, mostly running north and south. The population of the Colony, by the census taken in 1911, was 75,572, and of the Protectorate 1,327,560.

Administrative Divisions.—The country is divided into seven administrative districts, two of which are in the Colony and five in the Protectorate. The latter have been formed primarily in accordance with tribal settlements, due to the expediency of recognising in each the native customary law; the exception to this is the Railway district, in which other considerations of greater importance are involved.

Natural Features.—Although the country is largely of a slightly undulating type, in the north a curious formation of hills exists, in the Koinadugu district; each hill bearing a curiously-formed pinnacle of rock on its summit, and presenting a most striking appearance. The valleys between these hills contain some of the richest soil found in the country. Farther north, above the 9th degree of latitude, the country is composed chiefly of grass land interspersed with stunted trees. Approaching the coast, secondary forest or scrub occurs, which is constantly being cleared for farms; being so used for a year or two and then allowed to revert to "bush" for long periods.

Natives.—The inhabitants of the Colony are chiefly the descendants of liberated slaves from North America and the West Indies, but a number were rescued by British war-vessels from slave ships, and represent races from all parts of West Africa. The language adopted by these people is a "pidgin English" of a peculiar kind, and is easily understood after a few of the curious idiomatic phrases have been learnt.

The most important tribes are the Mendis, Timanis, Limbas and Sherbros. These are followed in number by the Konnohs, Port Lokkos, Susus, Korankos, Bulloms, Krims, Yalunkas, Mandingoes, Gbemas, Foulahs, Gallinas or Veis and Gpakas. The Mendis are the largest tribe, and are entirely pagan; they cultivate in a wasteful manner and are otherwise improvident. The Timanis are more intelligent and careful, and the Veis, occupying the sea coast to the south, who have recently adopted cocoa planting, are not only considered the most intelligent, but, alone among West African natives, have a written language.

Land Tenure.—The land in the Colony is held by the Crown, and is granted on the authority of the Governor. All grants made contain reservations with regard to roads and other public requirements. The tenure of Crown lands is fee simple, but occupation is also sanctioned under squatters' licence at a nominal rent, and the tenure is then in the nature of a tenancy at will. Under Ordinance No. 14 of 1886, real and personal property may be taken, acquired, held or disposed of by any alien in a manner similar to that allowed to a British-born subject.

Fields or waste lands outside town or village limits in the Sierra Leone Peninsula and Sherbro Island must be taken up in lots of not less than 20, or more than 200, acres. Such lots are disposed of at auction, at an upset price of 4*s*. 2*d*. per acre in the former, and 8*s*. in the latter locality. Up to 1902 the question of land grants in the Protectorate was unsettled, but arrangements may now be come to with the chiefs for the lease of tracts of land for long periods on an annual rental, agreed to between the applicant and the tribal council; the title requiring the confirmation of the Government. According to native law, it is generally recognised that the lands of a chiefdom are not the property of the chief, but are held in trust by him for the tribe. A chief has no power to alienate any portion of the land of a chiefdom, or to grant to any one perpetual rights to any portion, but the lease of land by an arrangement with the tribal council, and with the approval of Government, should be satisfactory for all requirements with regard to legal title.

Labour.—Plantations worked by chiefs at the instigation of Government are usually supplied with labour by the chief, although monetary assistance in the form of bonuses is occasionally given. Under such conditions experimental plantations of fibre, rubber, kola, etc., have been made. There is no fixed rate of pay for labourers, but the usual wage for an adult man, when hired, is from 6*d*. to 1*s*. per day.

Cultivation.—Throughout the country a shallow type of cultivation is common, and one in which the bush stumps and roots are not removed. The seeds of a number of different kinds of agricultural crops are generally mixed together before being sown broadcast over the lightly scraped soil of the burnt bush area.

The object of retaining the bush stumps and roots in the fields is that, after two or three years of cultivation, the bush may be easily reinstated, and again after ten or fifteen years, when cut down and burnt, it furnishes a supply of wood ash for the fertilisation of the field. This application of ash constitutes the only form of artificial renovation which the soil ever receives.

Recently experiments have been made in the presence of natives, in order to show the advantages of deep cultivation. To effect this, without the employment of ploughs, the fork kodalli hoe, recommended by the writer, has been introduced and generally adopted. The substantial increase in the production of their rice fields obtained by the use of this implement made a fortunate impression among the natives.

The native agricultural implements consist of a straight-handled, narrow-bladed hoe called "kari" (Mendi), or "katala" (Timani), and one formed from an angled stick with a charred point, called "baowe" (Mendi), or "kalal" (Timani). This last is used for drilling. In addition to these, a large broad-bladed hoe, called "karu wai" (Mendi), or "katala kabana" (Timani), is employed for cleaning out weeds and scraping the soil surface; the latter being the only cultivation the growing crop receives. These implements are illustrated below.

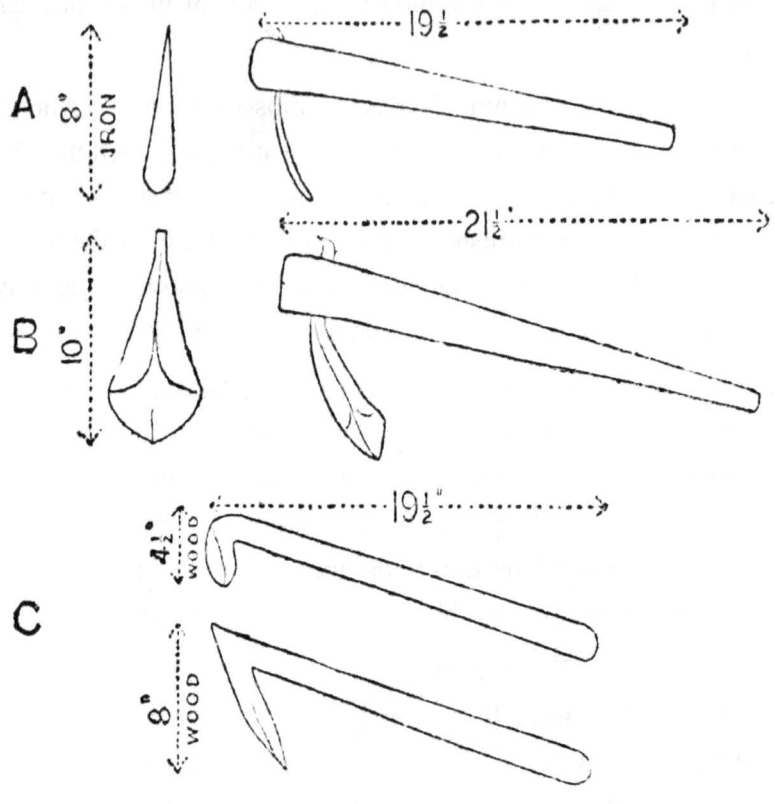

A. "KARI" (MENDI), "KATALA" (TIMANI).
B. "KAKU WAI" (MENDI), "KATALA KABANA" (TIMANI),
C. "BAOWE" (MENDI), "KALAL" (TIMANI).

Agricultural Schools, etc. *Chiefs' Sons' College.*—In 1906 a college for the sons of chiefs was established at Bo, and it was intended that, in addition to the ordinary course of instruction, the rudiments of improved agriculture should be taught. This was subsequently found to interfere with the teaching of other subjects which were considered more necessary, and was abandoned in consequence. The omission of agricultural training from the course did not preclude the scholars from cultivating small patches of vegetables for their own use, upon ground allowed to them for the purpose.

Thomas Agricultural College.—In 1908 the erection of an Agricultural College was commenced at Mabang, under the terms of the will of Mr. Thomas, a native who bequeathed a large sum of money to be devoted to this purpose. The College was expected to be completed in June 1910, when a commencement of lectures and general instruction was to be made. Scholarships and some official control were provided for by the terms of the trust, but the project was never developed, and the buildings were not even completed.

Principal Crops.—The most important food crop is rice, but two varieties of maize are also cultivated for local consumption; one of these is quick maturing, and is probably identical with the white variety which is exported from Lagos, from which country it is said to have been introduced into Sierra Leone. The other kind is of slower growth, and bears a yellow grain. Yams, sweet potatoes, and cassava are grown, especially where there is a heavy rainfall.

Forest Products.—Besides the agricultural crops, the forests yield palm oil and kernels, and kola nuts are planted for the much appreciated seed which their pods contain. The latter nut is said to have a stimulating effect, and to allay hunger and thirst when chewed. The nut is in such great demand throughout Northern Africa that a large trade exists between Sierra Leone and the coast countries to the north.

The more important exported products are accorded the foremost positions in the following account.

OIL PALM. Localities and the Influence of Position. *Elæis guineensis* is found generally throughout the country from the sea-board towards the interior, diminishing in those districts where the climate becomes drier or where rocky and mountainous tracts intervene. In places, owing, doubtless, to the wasteful methods of treatment and the carelessness in burning the "bush" for farms, extensive areas without palms are occasionally met with, even where the soil and climatic conditions are not unfavourable to their growth. In the extreme north, where the rainfall diminishes, the tree is only found in the vicinity of streams. The most suitable situation for growth seems to be one in which the soil is generally rather moist, although swampy, ill-drained land is not favourable. In those parts of the country where a gravelly laterite appears as a surface soil over a deep substratum of syenite, trees may often be met with in considerable numbers, but it is observed that the trunks of such trees do not acquire the same thickness as those growing in a damper and lighter soil. It is probable, although no experiments have yet been made affording direct evidence for the conclusion, that the fertility and yield of fruits of the trees growing upon the flat lands are greater than those established upon the higher undulating country because they are subject to less wash and more natural irrigation. It is also quite possible that the variety of palm fruit produced in the former places will be found to furnish better commercial results. No distinct varieties are, however, recognised by the natives, although distinctive names are applied to the same fruit in different stages of development.

The oil palm does not appear to be able to thrive in heavy forest, and in a natural state occupies open valleys with low undergrowth, but upon the clearance of primary forest it soon becomes established.

The seeds or nuts, which are large and heavy, are distributed by the agency of frugivorous birds and mammals. The grey parrot, for example, may be observed extracting the ripe fruits from the heads or picking them from the ground where they have fallen, and, after conveying these to a convenient tree, carefully removing the oily pericarp before dropping the nut in a new position. Monkeys doubtless convey the fruits to even greater distances in their cheek-pouches.

Owing to the presence of rocky and swampy strips of country in the Protectorate, and the direction in which farm fires have been carried by the prevailing winds, the distribution of palms has been thought to assume the character of "belts," defined by fairly well-marked boundaries. When looked into more closely, however, the distribution appears to be better described as consisting of dense patches linked sometimes by almost unrecognisable chains of widely scattered trees, and often broken into by short ranges of hills which are completely destitute of palms.

The patches referred to may bear 500 palm trees to the acre, and these may represent 80 to 100 per cent. of the total tree-growth on the patch. The area of such a patch may be roughly estimated at from ¼ acre to 15 sq. miles, or even more, but it should be added that, where such extensive tracts as these occur, the difficulties of transport and the scarcity of the population have constituted obstacles to working, and to the means of preserving the trees. Oil palms near Mafokoyia are shown in the picture (Fig. 10).

OIL PALMS (*ELÆIS GUINEENSIS*), MAFOKOYIA.
Fig. 10

NATIVE COLLECTING OIL PALM FRUIT, BLAMA.
Fig 11

KOLA TREE AT MANO.
Fig. 12

The appearance of a young tree is that of a thick stem throwing out annulate series of long feathery leaf fronds, upon petioles, which bear roughly-formed spines. As the tree increases in height the lower petioles are shed, and the trunk assumes a narrower but more regular form; indistinct rings being traceable, formed by the bases of the fallen leaf stems. A mature tree will measure about one foot in diameter at four feet from the ground, and at the ground surface the diameter will be two and a half to nearly three times as much. The male flowers are collected in the form of a number of tassel-like pendants, springing from a common stalk, and one such bunch is usually found above and upon each side of the female inflorescence. Both sexes of flowers usually occur upon the trees, but the natives recognise the existence of a non-fruiting tree, and one which only produces male flowers. The number of fruit heads and the weight of these vary according to the position, age, and treatment of the tree. An idea may be given of the fruitfulness of trees, from the accounts obtained from natives in different parts of the country. The palm has two fruiting seasons, one during the dry weather and another during the rainy season, the latter being generally the lighter crop. It is estimated that a tree in full bearing will yield from twelve to twenty fruiting heads in one year, each of a fairly large size. A younger tree may only produce four to eight heads, but usually of a larger size; and a tree of only five or six years old may give about the same number of heads, but of smaller dimensions. From very old trees small heads with fruits of a diminished size are obtained. The weight of a moderately large head will be about thirty pounds, and will contain about twelve hundred fruits weighing roughly 23 lbs. An illustration showing two fruiting heads is given (Fig. 9).

The ripe fruiting heads are gathered by a man using a climbing sling, with which he encircles the tree and his waist, and by means of a skilful manipulation of the part in contact with the trunk and remote from the body, he proceeds to ascend the tree rapidly, almost as though walking up it. On reaching the crown, a number of dead leaves have to be removed in order to get at the fruit stem. These are cut by means of a "cutlass" or "machete," which the climber carries, and are thrown to the ground. Only one head ripens at a time upon each tree, and the time occupied in climbing and cutting out the fruit head is estimated at about eight minutes. A photograph showing a native climbing a palm tree is reproduced (Fig. 11).

Both the Mendi and Timani races distinguish the fruit, at different periods during the advance towards maturity, by special names given with regard to the appearance. Identifications of the same series of fruits by different individuals have shown that these names are widely used.

Although it will be seen that in the Gold Coast and Nigeria the natives recognise a number of different varieties of fruit, this does not appear to be the case in Sierra Leone. The thin-shelled forms, so well known to the natives of the former countries, appear unknown, except around Sherbro, where there are a few trees recognised as productive of this type of fruit. In the appearance of the mature fruit, the presence or absence of black at the apex seems to be of equally common occurrence, but no importance is attached to this feature.

The Sierra Leone form appears to be at a disadvantage with regard to the proportion of oily pericarp covering the nut, as well as in the great thickness of its shell. Comparing it with the varieties obtained in the Gold Coast, it is probably nearest to, if not identical with, that called "Abe pa."

When the percentage of oil extracted from the fruit of the Sierra Leone trees is compared with that from other parts of West Africa, it at once becomes apparent that the amount is small. The results of three series of experiments, made in different parts of the country, showed that the fibrous pericarp, which contains the oil, constituted only about 30 per cent. of the whole, the nut containing the kernel being large and approximating 70 per cent. Palm oil extracted by native methods gave 1·201, 5·47, 5·637, and 8·326 per cent. respectively in four tests. If these results are compared with the extractions of oil from the several Gold

Coast varieties, the deficiency is very marked. Compare *Bulletin of the Imperial Institute*, vol. vii. (1909), pp. 364-71.

A close examination of the local fruit shows that the outer fibrous portion or pericarp, which alone contains the palm oil, is very thin, whereas the hard shell surrounding the kernel is thick. The kernel represents about 15 per cent. of the total weight of the fruit, and is largely exported from the country for the extraction of another kind of oil.

Small Export of Oil compared with Kernels.—The proportionately larger weight of kernel than of palm oil capable of extraction, accounts for the large quantities of kernels exported compared with palm oil. As an example of this, it may be mentioned that in the year 1906 Sierra Leone exported only 12½ gallons of palm oil to each ton of kernels, whereas Southern Nigeria figures for the same year showed 142 gallons of oil per ton of kernels. Since this date, up to the beginning of the war, a comparison of the annual exports of oil and kernels shows a fluctuation between about 12 and 19 gallons of pericarp oil for every ton of kernels; the latter still remaining disproportionately high.

Proposal to introduce New Varieties.—Since it has begun to be realised that the local variety of palm is probably constantly inferior as an oil producer to some of the varieties found farther to the south, it has been suggested that some of the forms, with a thicker fibrous pericarp and a thin-shelled kernel, should be introduced and planted upon an extensive scale. It is assumed that by doing so, a better type would become established. Experiments made in the Kamerun show, however, that the progeny of palms having a thin-shelled fruit (Lisombe) do not necessarily retain their important characters. Dr. Strunk has suggested that, in the variety mentioned, the characters are not fixed or susceptible of transmission, but the experiments are not considered as yielding conclusive evidence, and it is advisable that experimental plots should be planted with the more useful forms in Sierra Leone and elsewhere, the seed being obtained from artificially fertilised sources.

Improvements in the Local Manufacture.—During recent years great efforts have been made by the Administration to increase the exports of both palm oil and kernels by opening up the previously rather inaccessible areas in which palm trees were found growing almost untouched. The first step in this direction was the extension of the Sierra Leone Railway line from Boia, a small village just beyond the Headquarters District boundary, to Mafokoyia, lying a short distance to the north. From here a road was made eastwards towards Yonnibannah, passing through country fairly well studded with oil palms. Later from Yonnibannah the objective of the railway became Baga, a town on the Maybole river, again to the north. At the present time this line has reached Kamabai, at the foot of the Koinadugu mountains and to the west of Bumban, passing the town of Makump on its way there. The whole of this route has been chosen in order to make the oil palm regions more accessible, and the increase in exports of both oil and kernels between 1907 and 1913 is almost entirely attributable to this development.

Not only was it desirable to open up new areas from which palm fruits could be gathered, but, owing to the deficiency of pericarp oil shipped from the country in comparison with palm kernels, it was thought that, by the introduction of improved methods for extracting the pericarp oil, more of this commodity might be obtainable in the future.

The prospect of working a large area both experimentally and commercially for oil extraction *in situ*, attracted Messrs. Lever Brothers, who installed ample mechanical apparatus at Yonnibannah in 1914. The Government had granted this firm a concession to work several hundred square miles on the understanding that the local traders and merchants were not thereby to be debarred from buying the hand-prepared oil from the natives as before. The scheme was intended to demonstrate the advantages of mechanical means of extraction over those of hand power; and it was thought that, by the introduction of these greater facilities for dealing with the oil palm products, labour would be liberated and would be employed to a greater extent in the less heavy and more remunerative direction of plantation and field work. Messrs. Lever Brothers' factory was one designed to be equipped both from a mechanical and research standpoint, and a special shunting yard on the railway was leased to the firm by the Government to deal with the anticipated work. The project seemed so promising that local firms were contemplating following Messrs. Lever Brothers' example in other localities. The whole scheme was, however, abandoned after a short trial; Messrs. Lever Brothers having probably discovered two facts in connection with the oil palm industry in Sierra Leone which had been lost sight of. The first is that the pericarp of the common type of palm fruit found in Sierra Leone, as pointed out in the first edition of this book, is very thin and therefore contains very little oil, and that the shell of the nuts in this thin-pericarped fruit is extremely thick. The common Sierra Leone kind is therefore of less economic value both in respect to pericarp oil and kernel contents than the common kind found in the Gold Coast, Nigeria and Kamerun. The second point is that the Mendis and Timanis occupying this part of the Protectorate are a lower type and generally poorer workers by comparison with the Fanti tribes of the Gold Coast or the Yorubas of Nigeria.

One explanation given for the failure of Messrs. Lever Brothers' effort in Sierra Leone was that they did not offer a sufficiently high price for the oil palm fruit heads to induce the natives to collect and carry them to the factory. As the chiefs and villagers saw that by selling the fruits to the factory the main occupation of their wives (the preparation of palm oil and the cracking of nuts for the extraction of palm kernels) would be taken away, they were said to be averse to the establishment of a new condition of enforced idleness, which would impose greater difficulties on them of keeping their wives in order. The offer by the factory to return the nuts for cracking in the villages, did not dispose of this difficulty, as the villagers only saw in it an arrangement involving them in extra transport. Messrs. Lever Brothers have now transferred their work to the Belgian Congo, where, by reason of the better type of palm fruit commonly obtainable, the conditions are more satisfactory for the development of the mechanical extraction of palm oil on a commercial scale, and where the inhabitants are less independent and more accustomed to co-operate with European enterprise.

Export Figures.—The average annual export of palm oil and kernels for the first nine years of the century, and the annual total of the subsequent ten years are given:

Year	Palm oil Gallons	Palm kernels Tons
1900-1908 Av.	303,790	26,630
1909	851,998	42,897
1910	645,339	43,031

1911	725,648	42,892
1912	728,509	50,751
1913	617,088	49,201
1914	436,144	35,915
1915	481,576	39,624
1916	557,751	45,316
1917	543,111	58,020
1918	260,442	40,816

RUBBER.—Until 1907 the African tree rubber (*Funtumia elastica*) had not been recorded from any part of the country, although its congener, *F. africana*, was found everywhere. A number of trees of the first-named species have been recently discovered in the Panguma and Gola forests, and have been carefully examined. The latex, from trees tapped in the former locality, yielded a good quality of rubber when boiled with three volumes of water.

Native Method of Preparation.—The tree is known to the Mendis as "Gboi-gboi," and in order to obtain the latex it is customary to fell the tree, afterwards ringing it at intervals of about one foot. The latex, which flows, is collected in leaf cups or other receptacles, and is heated in an iron pot. When in a state of semi-coagulation, induced by heat, it is poured upon plantain leaves, placed on the ground. Another plantain leaf is then used to cover the mass, which is stamped out with the feet into a rough sheet. The sheet is hung up to dry in a hut, in which it obtains the benefit of the fumes from the wood fires used by the occupants. The next process is to cut the sheet into strips, which are subsequently wound into large oval balls and enter the Freetown market under the name of "Manoh twist."

Owing to the wasteful method of tapping the trees, the species has been exterminated in many places, and the local Government have had under consideration the formulation of an ordinance to prevent the continuance of such destruction. As the existing trees are now practically only found in the dense forests near the Liberian frontier, and are probably widely scattered over a large area, it will prove a difficult matter to enforce any regulations with regard to collection.

Vine Rubber: Method of Preparation.—*Landolphia owariensis*, var. *Jenje*, is said to be the species of vine from which the Sierra Leone "Red Nigger" rubber is obtained. The Mendi name for the plant is "Djenje." A very destructive method is usually employed in the preparation of the rubber. The vine is cut down and the roots dug out, both of which are cut into small pieces and soaked in water for several weeks. The bark is then removed, and the wood is pounded and washed repeatedly until a reddish mass of rubber remains, which usually contains a large amount of woody matter. This is sold in the form of balls. It is less common for the native to tap the vine and to coagulate the latex upon the wound with the addition of salt or lime juice, but this is occasionally done, and balls of scrap rubber collected in this way are sold in some localities.

Another vine (*Clitandra laxiflora*), which yields an inferior rubber by means of boiling the latex, is termed "Jawe" by the Mendis. This was at first considered to be *Clitandra Manni*, but more recent investigation has proved that *C. Manni*, although called by the same native name, produces a latex incapable of coagulation.

The Quality of Indigenous Rubbers and the Export.—The prices obtained for Sierra Leone rubbers compare favourably with those of the other British West African countries. Funtumia rubber, which is generally largely adulterated in the Gold Coast and Nigeria, is apparently not so in Sierra Leone, when prepared in the form of "Manoh twist." The vine rubber, made from the scrap, is also of good quality, and the root rubber is not inferior to that shipped from the other countries. The trade of Sierra Leone is, however, small, and it is probable that the larger part of that exported from Freetown is obtained from the adjoining countries of Liberia and French Guinea. The export of rubber declined since 1906, when it amounted to 107 tons, to only 6 tons in 1913, while in 1916 and 1917 none was exported. The composition and quality of Sierra Leone rubbers is given in the *Bulletin of the Imperial Institute*, vol. iv. (1906), p. 29; vol. vi. (1908), p. 24; vol. viii. (1910), p. 16; and vol. xii. (1914), p. 371.

Rubber Plantations.—No plantations of Funtumia rubber have been made although small plots have been planted with the South American Para tree (*Hevea brasiliensis*) on an experimental scale at different times and in various parts of the country and a mixed plantation of rubber, cocoa, coffee and fruit has been made near Waterloo. Up to 1909, it should be remarked, the work was in the hands of the Agricultural Service, but from 1910, on the formation of the Forestry Department as well as the reorganisation of an Agricultural Department, all forest and plantation work was transferred to the first-named Department. No plantation rubber has yet reached the commercial stage, although further trials are still in progress, and much experience has been gained.

A few Para trees were planted at the beginning of the present century in the Botanic Gardens at Freetown, but the locality was found unsuitable, and the trees grew slowly and yielded unsatisfactorily. A small plantation was made at Moyamba by Madam Yoko, the late chief of the Mendis, and was well looked after until she died, since when it seems to have been somewhat neglected. At Mano, the chief of the town made a good plantation in 1906, and, as the locality was apparently well selected, the trees have shown satisfactory growth. Small plots have been put out under Para at the Roman Catholic Mission station at Serabu, at Segbwema, Tinainahun and the Bo school, with variable success, in accordance with the cultivation and care bestowed on the plants. Except in the gravelly positions the tree succeeds well.

Landolphia owariensis and *L. Heudelotii* have been planted in forested patches in different parts of the country, the supervision of such planting having been entrusted to a native who had seen similar work performed by the French authorities in the neighbouring colony. Near Batkanu, a few plants can still be seen.

KOLA NUTS.—The importance of the kola nut in West Africa is very high. Sierra Leone produces generally a better quality, for local consumption and export, than other countries. The kola trees (*Kola acuminata* and *K. vera*) do not, however, occur in a wild state in the country, and the whole produce is obtained from plantations, which are to be seen near almost every village in the moist region. A photograph is given showing a kola tree at Mano (Fig. 12). The destination of the exported kola is chiefly Bathurst (Gambia), Dakar (Senegal), Bissao (Portuguese Guinea), and to a small extent Dahomey. The exports of this commodity in recent years are given below as well as their average annual values per ton, which, as will be seen, exhibit great fluctuation.

	Tons	Valued at	Equal to £ per ton
1906	1,155	£104,084	£90
1907	1,374	£113,674	£83
1908	1,162	£108,895	£94

1909	1,320	£153,848	£116
1910	1,508	£191,878	£127
1911	1,597	£194,260	£121
1912	1,649	£276,473	£167
1913	1,865	£328,003	£176
1914	1,924	£279,185	£145
1915	2,041	£233,388	£119
1916	2,484	£302,720	£122
1917	1,702	£321,105	£188
1918	2,302	£397,726	£173

Kola nuts are second only to palm kernels in Sierra Leone in importance as an export, although they are practically entirely consigned to other coast ports; an insignificant amount of dried kolas only being destined for Europe.

RED PEPPER.—*Capsicum annuum* and *C. frutescens* are both grown among the multitude of plants, the seeds of which are mixed and broadcasted in the farms; but whereas most of the other plants are annuals, these are left in the ground for two years or more, and yield almost continuous crops during that period. The country of origin of these plants is probably South America, but the date of their introduction is unknown.

Beside the extensive local use of the pods, the export statistics of 1909 show that 41 tons were shipped.

GINGER.—*Zingiber officinale* is not found in a wild state in Africa, but has been widely introduced throughout the tropical portions, although in Sierra Leone, alone among the West African countries, has it reached the important position of an export.

Owing to the defective methods of agriculture employed in the Colony, where for the most part ginger is cultivated, the roots or rhizomes do not attain a large size, and, in consequence, present great difficulties in decortication.

The common native method of preparation is to rub the washed and partially dried rhizomes in sand, and then to dry them more or less completely in the sun. The effect of this treatment is to remove a small portion of the outer skin from those prominences which come into contact with the sandy surface more readily, the depressions being left untouched. The native has found that the weight of the prepared ginger is increased by the adhesion of sand, and therefore prefers to employ this method to that of using a knife. The result is a very inferior product.

During the last few years attempts have been made among the ginger growers to deal directly with the European buyers, and a Farmers' Association was formed with this object in view. Government assistance was obtained on the assurance that better methods of cultivation and preparation would be adopted, and this was done to a certain extent, but greater dependence seems to have been placed upon the supposed advantage to be obtained from shipping ginger of the usual inferior quality, without it passing through the local merchants' hands. The result was, that a small quantity of selected ginger was sold at a good price, and a large quantity of common grade obtained a lower price than previously.

Recent experiments have shown that good results can be obtained with ginger in Sierra Leone if care be taken to deep-hoe the ground and then plant out the selected eyes from clean rhizomes. The custom of attempting to grow a crop in hard laterite gravel without proper cultivation is the chief cause of the malformed and small rhizomes usually obtained in native cultivation. Under improved conditions a crop of five tons per acre of good quality ginger has been procured.

Export Trade.—The following amounts of ginger have been shipped during the last decade:

	Tons	Value		Tons	Value
1906	579	10,879	1913	2,048	35,468
1907	618	11,578	1914	1,213	15,639
1908	637	11,871	1915	567	8,091
1909	722	14,147	1916	971	25,814
1910	1,093	33,288	1917	1,136	25,863
1911	1,692	44,668	1918	1,576	39,306
1912	2,200	44,864			

It is reported that, owing to the decline in price paid for Sierra Leone ginger in 1913, about one-third of the crop was left unharvested, and that the depreciation experienced was due to the competition from other sources of a better marketed product. It would be a pity if the promising opportunity of the country to become established as a large producer of ginger were altogether lost, owing to the want of a little care in cultivation and preparation of the product for the market.

The plant is essentially suited to certain parts of the Colony and Protectorate and is not subject to any serious diseases, the only recorded one being a fungus which attacks the rhizomes and causes yellowing of the leaves. This can be prevented from spreading if the plants be removed and burned as soon as the signs of attack are apparent on them.

FIBRES. Jute Class.—In the last few years several fibre plants indigenous to the country have been experimented with at the Imperial Institute, in order to ascertain whether any were capable of being exported for use as substitutes for Indian jute.

Honckenyaficifolia, known by the Timani name of "Napunti," a plant which occurs in great profusion in the swamps and low lands, yields a fibre of excellent quality, but owing to the difficulties experienced in the extraction of it, further experiments are necessary to devise a means by which it can be economically prepared. The analyses of the fibre from this plant which have been made at the Imperial Institute (see *Selected Reports from the Imperial Institute*, Part I. [Cd. 4588], Fibres, p. 40) are very satisfactory, and this, combined with the fact that the natural supply of the plant is very large in districts which are quite useless for agricultural purposes, renders it important that the methods of extraction should be more carefully studied.

Among the other fibres of this class which have shown promise, *Hibiscus quinquelobus*, to which the Mendis give the name of "Korwey," is found in a wild state in variable profusion throughout the country. Unlike the last, which produces erect stems growing close together, this plant has stems of an almost scandent character, growing under the shade of moderately large trees and perforating the upper branches, so that the flowering stems are often seen fifteen feet or more above the ground. Under cultivation the experiments seemed to show that the elongated character of the stems was not maintained, and this defect requires to be remedied if the fibre is to be prepared upon a commercial scale. The extraction is easily done by retting, and experimental shipments to Europe of several tons have shown that the product is quite marketable and is classed with, or a little below, medium jutes (*ibid.* p. 39).

Recently experiments were carried out in the extraction of

fibre from *Hibiscus esculentus*, the "okra" of tropical countries. A specimen of the fibre having been examined at the Imperial Institute and favourably reported upon (*ibid.* p. 35), a plantation was made at Kangahun, in order to endeavour to produce a crop, which should have the additional advantage of yielding a marketable supply of the vegetable okra pods before being cut down and made into fibre. In order to do this, the seed was sown at close intervals, thereby introducing a straight growth of stem, and care was exercised not to permit the fruiting to continue long enough for the stems to become coarse. The fibre was extracted in the same manner as that of jute, except that the stems were immersed in a solution of caustic soda before retting to remove the thin outer bark. The marketed fibre from the first of these experiments realised an unsatisfactory price, but it was estimated that the crop of pods yielded £3 per acre.

Corchorus capsularis, one of the Indian jutes, was introduced and planted out in 1906, but the existing native methods of cultivation and the absence of manure rendered the conditions so different from those obtained in India, that a successful result was not brought about. Two species of Corchorus are found in the country, and are used only as vegetables.

Ramie Fibre.—Plantations of Ramie fibre or China grass were recently made in various parts of the Protectorate, but although the plant grows well during the rainy season, the long period of dry weather is detrimental to it.

Piassava.—This fibre is produced from the sheath of the leaf stem of *Raphia vinifera*, the wine palm, and is prepared at several places, especially in the swampy districts near the coast. The method of extraction is merely that of steeping and beating out, and the resulting fibre is, in appearance, somewhat similar to fine whalebone. The largest amount was exported in 1915, when the figure reached 1,283 tons. The price in this year attained £61 per ton. The fibre is chiefly employed for the manufacture of stiff brooms.

COTTON.—The native cotton of Sierra Leone showed promise, at one time, of great development, but insurmountable difficulties met the efforts of the British Cotton Growing Association in their attempt to establish cotton growing for export upon a large scale.

The native mode of growing cotton is in combination with a number of other agricultural crops, the seeds of all being mixed before being broadcasted in a field, which has been lightly tilled. Cotton sown in this manner is permitted to yield crops for two seasons, but the second crop is generally much inferior. Owing to this irregular manner of planting, the amount of cotton available for use is small, and is nearly all absorbed for the supply of the native looms; being readily saleable in the weaving districts at about $2d.$ per lb. of seed cotton, or about twice as much as the British Cotton Growing Association were prepared to pay.

The inefficiency of the quality of the local cultivation, and the disinclination on the part of the native to adopt better methods, effectually prevented more cotton being grown, and the British Cotton Growing Association were unable to obtain sufficient material to keep their ginnery employed.

In connection with the cotton ginnery, erected at Moyamba, a large plantation was made; the indigenous as well as many exotic varieties of the plant being put in. The site, however, proved unsuitable, labour was found to be expensive, and the climatic conditions were complained of. In consequence of these adverse conditions, the Association were reluctantly obliged to abandon the work. The export of cotton was never significant and ceased altogether in 1909.

Indigenous Varieties.—Three well-marked types of cotton are found throughout the country, and are known by the native (Mendi) names of (1) Kwonde, (2) Fande Wa, (3) Dhoole. The first of these has a white lint and a seed covered with white wool. An examination of this at the Imperial Institute showed that the lint from it was the most valuable of the three; the staple measured about 1″, and was compared with very good quality "Indian Broach." Two samples, valued in 1907, were priced at 5⅜d. and 5¾d. respectively, with good Broach at 5⅜d., and Middling American at 6·18d. The Fande Wa variety has a creamy lint and a green woolly seed. It was said to be of good quality, but the colour was not so good as the last, and the value was consequently lower. Dhoole is rather rarer than the other two, and has a brick-red or brown lint and a bare seed. Khaki or red cottons are not in demand upon an European market, but locally they are somewhat sought after.

Native Weaving.—A native cloth woven from the three different varieties of indigenous cottons is frequently seen; the careful arrangement of the naturally coloured yarns yielding a distinct pattern. More often, perhaps, only the first two kinds are used, and the yarn made from them is dyed with the local indigo. In width the native cloths are usually narrow, and the strips are sewn together in order to form gowns, etc. A photograph is given showing a native weaver at work at Pendembu (Fig. 13). In a few localities wider cloths are woven, but of no great length. These are often elaborately designed, and command a high price among the natives, being preferred to imported materials.

Exotic Cottons.—"Cambodia" and "Sea Island" have been

tried experimentally. The latter, though withstanding the heavy rainfall well, was found to be very susceptible to attacks of the local cotton stainer. There is still no prospect of the revival of cotton exportation.

NATIVE WEAVER AT PENDEMBU.
Fig. 13

KUMASSI, THE CAPITAL OF ASHANTI.
Fig. 14

STONE VAT FOR POUNDING PALM FRUITS, WITH SURROUNDING GUTTER AND OIL WELL, KROBO PLANTATIONS.
Fig. 15

RICE.—Two forms of rice are grown in the Protectorate; one under irrigation or in swampy ground, near rivers, etc., and the other entirely without any conservance of water, depending on the rainfall.

The use of rice is general throughout the country—in fact, it is probably the most important food crop; and although, as mentioned above, there are two forms, divided according to their mode of cultivation, each form contains many varieties distinguished by different native names.

In the Timani country and the vicinity of Port Lokko the finest quality is grown, and the husking of this is said to be a prolonged process of drying, without previously parboiling or soaking. This rice only requires to be thoroughly dried before the husk will separate on pounding.

In the Mendi country, the heads of rice at the harvesting are cut and tied in small bunches to dry in the fields. The grain is then beaten out, and the chaff winnowed on a tray or in a gentle breeze. The next step is to parboil the grain while yet in the husk, during which operation the interior swells up so as to split the husk. The rice is then again thoroughly dried in the sun upon mats, and finally lightly pounded in a wooden mortar in order to separate the loosened husk, which is removed by winnowing. From the time of harvesting until the rice is ready for sale, the work is performed by women.

In spite of the fact that a very large quantity of rice is grown, it frequently happens that in a good season much remains unharvested, owing to the improvidence of the native. The price just after harvesting may fall as low as 1*s*. 6*d*. per bushel, but a few months later it may reach three times that amount. It is customary for the Protectorate native to realise at once upon his crop, without taking the precaution to lay in a store for his future requirements. In consequence of this he is compelled to buy back supplies for his own consumption at a very much enhanced rate. The native at the Coast takes advantage of this improvidence and profits considerably by it; buying up the cheap product at harvesting and realising a handsome profit after a few months.

In quality the local rice is excellent, but in appearance it is somewhat reddish, only a few of the finer qualities being nearly white. The imported rices are usually white, but are said to contain less nutriment than the local kinds.

Rice has always constituted the staple food of the aboriginal tribes of the Protectorate, for which reason its cultivation and the weather conditions necessary for its successful production locally are matters of great importance. No precaution is taken to plant any other crop as a stand-by in the event of an unfavourable rice season. In 1910 a disaster actually occurred, for the rainy season of 1909 set in so early that it prevented many farms being burned in time to sow rice. Most of the local varieties mature their grain from three to five months after sowing, the earlier producing approximately 15, and the later from 30 to 40 bushels, per acre. Owing to the failure of the rice crop in 1910, the commodity should not have been allowed to be exported in that year, but the importance of this was lost sight of in view of the remunerative trade in it which had become established with different coast ports to which it was shipped. In the previous edition of this volume a recommendation was made to foster the export of surplus Sierra Leone rice to the Gold Coast, where it was much appreciated, and doubtless this trade may yet become important when existing restrictions are removed, and if it is found possible to induce a larger number of the population in the Protectorate to engage in pure agriculture, and grow crops in excess of their immediate personal requirements.

The exports for the last nine years were as follows:

	Bushels	Value £
1910	35,114	5,925
1911	22,621	4,716
1912	30,715	5,712
1913	21,548	3,991
1914	18,705	4,855
1915	19,600	7,228
1916	3,192	1,364
1917	1,022	697
1918	176	93

In 1915, owing to the falling off of imports, it was found necessary to exercise control over the exports, but in spite of this the amount exported was higher than in the previous year. In 1916 the urgency of the matter became even more pronounced and exports were restricted.

The Agricultural Department conducted several comparative trials with Indian and local varieties of rice. The Indian rices were much smaller in size of grain and were generally not considered so suitable as the local kinds, with respect to which it was found that, with a sufficiency of seed used in sowing and deep cultivation, excellent crops could be secured. The native method of using less than half a bushel of seed to sow an acre is accountable for much of the resultant crop becoming full of weeds. Excellent results were obtained in sowing 1½ to 3 bushels per acre, when the weeds were choked out.

CAMWOOD.—This material, from which red dye is got, is obtained from the leguminous tree *Baphia nitida*. The use of it in European countries has somewhat diminished during recent years, owing to the substitution for it of artificial red colouring-matter, but a small quantity is still exported, and is made use of for colouring sausage skins. The amount of camwood exported in 1915 is given as 635 tons, valued at £8,761.

COPAL.—The tree identified as *Copaifera Guibourtiana* is tapped, in the Mendi country especially, for copal. The method in general practice is to cut small square patches of bark from the main trunk and branches in the month of January, and to permit these to exude resin until April, at which time the flow has ceased, and the resin hardened sufficiently to be collected.

The tree has been recorded from a few localities in Sierra Leone, but recently plantations have been made near Moyamba and elsewhere. In the Kwalu district, where clusters of large trees occur, much damage has been done by overtapping, and many dead trees are to be seen.

The value of Sierra Leone copal is high, sometimes attaining over two shillings a pound in the European markets. The quality is, however, somewhat irregular, and the local grading is frequently inefficient. Information as to the quality and value of Sierra Leone copal in comparison with other varieties is given in *Selected Reports from the Imperial Institute*, Part II., Gums and Resins [Cd. 4971], pp. 170-82.

About thirty tons were annually shipped to Europe for making varnish, but owing to the destructive methods of collection, the Government has prohibited trade for five years.

GROUNDNUTS.—Practically no trade at present exists in this crop, but efforts are being made to reintroduce the cultivation into Bullom, where at one time a large quantity was grown for export.

The cultivation of groundnuts for local consumption is carried on, but the ridge system of planting, which is in vogue in the Gambia, is not adopted in Sierra Leone, and the groundnut stalks are removed from the ground without the nuts attached to them. The nuts in Sierra Leone are permitted to remain in the ground and depreciate in quality through insufficient drying. The success of groundnut cultivation depends largely upon the plant being grown on a loose bed of friable soil, and, where such conditions exist, the Gambian method should prove satisfactory.

Experiments show that the nuts should be decorticated before sowing. The usual local method of sowing is to scatter the nuts upon the unbroken ground and then cover with loose earth. Some damage is done by rats, bushpig and termites, and in 1914 a fungoid disease (*Cercospora personata*) appeared in Karene. The Agricultural Department has obtained 12 cwts. to the acre in its trials.

The variety of nut grown is apparently identical with that

of the Gambia, from which country the seed has probably been obtained in the past.

COCOA.—Some years ago cocoa was introduced into the Colony, but, although some of the Colonial planters had received their training in the cocoa estates of Fernando Po and San Thomé, no success attended their efforts in Sierra Leone. The heavy rainfall, combined with the long period of drought peculiar to the country, is detrimental to the industry. More recently experiments have been conducted in the Protectorate, where a lighter rainfall occurs; but here also the conditions are not generally favourable, as the long period of dry weather is not compensated for by humidity in the atmosphere.

Importance of Correct Climatic Conditions.—Cocoa plantations, in order to be successful, require atmospheric moisture fairly constantly throughout the year, and will not thrive if exposed to excessive and prolonged drought, or too much rain. Meteorological records taken at Bo, a place not far distant from that where cocoa experiments were made, show that the conditions in respect to distribution of rainfall, humidity and temperature are unfavourable there. Many attempts have been made in other localities, but only in Northern Sherbro has there been any appreciable success. The soil in this locality is deep and is kept in good tilth by the Gallinas. The price obtained locally for their cocoa beans was, in 1913, from $3d.$ to $4d.$ per lb.; in 1914 there was an increase in the number of plants put out, as the price rose in that year to $6d.$ per lb. A sample of native cocoa was submitted to the Imperial Institute for examination and report in 1916, and was found to be incompletely fermented with a rather harsh flavour. The trade valuation, however, was equal to the standard price ruling for Accra beans at the same time (cf. *Bull. Imp. Inst.*, 1916, p. 589). Although the outlook for Northern Sherbro is promising, cocoa cannot attain much success in the country generally, on account of unsuitable climatic conditions and general ineptitude of most of the native tribes.

COFFEE.—A few years ago coffee was grown in the Colony for export, the indigenous variety, *Coffea stenophylla* as well as *C. Liberica* being planted. The former bears a very small berry and yields an excellent, strong-flavoured beverage. The latter is better known and has a large berry. Throughout the hill villages of the Colony a great number of trees are seen, but, owing to a fall in the price of the product, most of the crop remains unpicked, although it should not prove unremunerative even at the present prices to continue the export.

INDIGO.—Species of Indigofera and a scandent shrub, *Lonchocarpus cyanescens*, or "Gara" (Mendi), are used for the extraction of the blue dyes commonly employed in the country. The leaves of the latter plant are said to be in such demand that a quantity is annually imported from Southern Nigeria. A description of the method of dyeing with "Gara," and an explanation of the process, are given in the *Bulletin of the Imperial Institute*, vol. v. (1907), p. 129.

FRUIT.—Some parts of the Colony seem favourable for the cultivation of various tropical fruits, such as bananas, oranges, mangoes, and pineapples, and it is possible that the proximity of Sierra Leone to European ports might enable some of these to be grown for export.

BEESWAX.—A small amount of beeswax is collected in the Protectorate, and instruction has been given to the natives in some localities with a view to the improvement of the methods employed by them. The Government has arranged for the instruction of some of the local officials while on leave in England in practical bee-keeping.

The bee found in Sierra Leone is identical with the variety of *Apis mellifera* found throughout West Africa, and is named var. *Adansonii*. It is rather small, but produces an excellent honey, which is much appreciated.

OIL SEEDS.—A tall tree bearing a large flattened legume, known to the Mendi people as "Fai," or "Fawe," has been sent for examination to the Imperial Institute on account of the oil contained in the seed. This tree was identified as *Pentaclethra macrophylla*, and, although common throughout the forested zone, is not seen in profusion anywhere. The oil has been tested, and is said to be capable of utilisation for the manufacture of soap and candles, but not for alimentary purposes. The difficulties in connection with the collection of the seed in large quantities and the extraction of the kernel from the outer horny shell, hinder the creation of a remunerative export trade.

Another vegetable oil is that obtained from the fruit of *Pentadesma butyracea*, a tree found in some parts of Bullom and in the Port Lokko district. The fat extracted from the ripe fruit is occasionally brought for sale to Freetown, where it is known as Mandingo butter. It does not occur in sufficient quantities to be commercially useful, although it yields an edible oil.

Lophira alata, which is widely distributed throughout the grass country in the north, and is replaced by a nearly allied species, *L. procera*, in the forest zone, bears a seed which contains a large percentage of oil, which can be used for soap manufacture. The difficulty of decorticating the seeds and their preservation during transport are disadvantages in the establishment of an export trade.

Analyses of the fats or oils yielded by these and other West African oil seeds, and information as to their quality, possible uses and value will be found in *Selected Reports from the Imperial Institute*, Pt. V., Oil Seeds (cf. also *Bull. Imp. Inst.*, 1912, 1913, 1915, 1917, 1918).

Progress in Agriculture.—In 1910 the Agricultural Department was reorganised on a better basis than formerly, and the purely forestry work, which had been previously carried on by the Agricultural Superintendent, in addition to his other duties, was then transferred to a Forestry Department formed in that year.

Briefly, the scheme of work laid down by the new Department of Agriculture may be said to be on the following chief lines:

(i) The introduction of a cheap and effective organic manure, and the demonstration of its value in such a manner as to induce the people to use it on their land, and thereby to employ more economical means for the production of food, etc.

(ii) The institution of a proper rotation of crops suitable for each district or locality.

(iii) The demonstration to natives of the fact, that, by the proper employment of manuring and crop rotation, they would be able to farm the same piece of land for an indefinite number of years, during which time it should increase rather than diminish in fertility. By such demonstration it should be possible to put an end to the wasteful and permanently destructive methods at present employed of shifting cultivation.

The Agricultural Department has a piece of land on the

Experiment Farm at Njala, which has been under crops annually for the past eight years, and the condition of it at present is said to be a more fertile one, owing to the system of manuring and rotation employed, than it was at the commencement of work. This is mentioned here, as it is in contradiction to the well-worn native excuse for changing the site of farms annually, *i.e.*, that it is essential for the maintenance of the fertility of land that after a few years' cultivation the "bush" be allowed to become re-established so that, on burning, a sufficient amount of wood ash may be obtained to renovate it.

(iv) To encourage the natives in the formation of permanent plantations of fruit and other economic trees.

To these ends, in the first place, analyses of soils from various parts of the country have been made by the Imperial Institute. At the same time samples of the soil taken from localities where kola, cocoa, rice and groundnuts were grown, have been compared with that from uncleared "bush." The result of the examination, in the latter case, showed the soil had a deficiency of lime and phosphoric acid. A special analysis was also made of the soil of the Banana Islands, which was found to have an adequate quantity of nitrogen but to be deficient in potash and phosphoric acid.

With a view to producing a more satisfactory condition of soil in some parts, different leguminous crops have been cultivated and alternated with Sorghum millet (Guinea corn), maize and rice. Among the species tried by the Agricultural Department are: soya beans (*Glycine soja*), black gram (*Phaseolus mungo*), pigeon peas (*Cajanus indicus*), Java beans (*Phaseolus lunatus*), cowpeas (*Vigna catjang*), sword beans (*Canavalia ensiformis*) and horse-beans (*Dolichos lablab*). Yams and groundnuts have also been tried, and a yield of 6 tons 3 cwts. per acre of the former crop was obtained at the experimental farm at Njala in 1914.

Forestry.—On the formation of a Forestry Department in 1910, a survey was at once proceeded with, and active steps were taken to save from extinction the small extent of forest remaining in the Colony and Protectorate. From the survey it appeared that some 99 per cent. of the Protectorate primary forest had already been destroyed by the wasteful methods of farming generally practised. Intervals between the clearing of the bush for farms was from nine to five years, the effect of which was to entirely eliminate the primary forest areas. Where patches still remain, however, many useful species of timber trees are found. By the introduction of regular forest control and reafforestation, it is hoped that conditions may be improved to some extent, and economic trees especially preserved. Forest legislation has already been introduced to insure the preservation of copal trees.

GOLD COAST

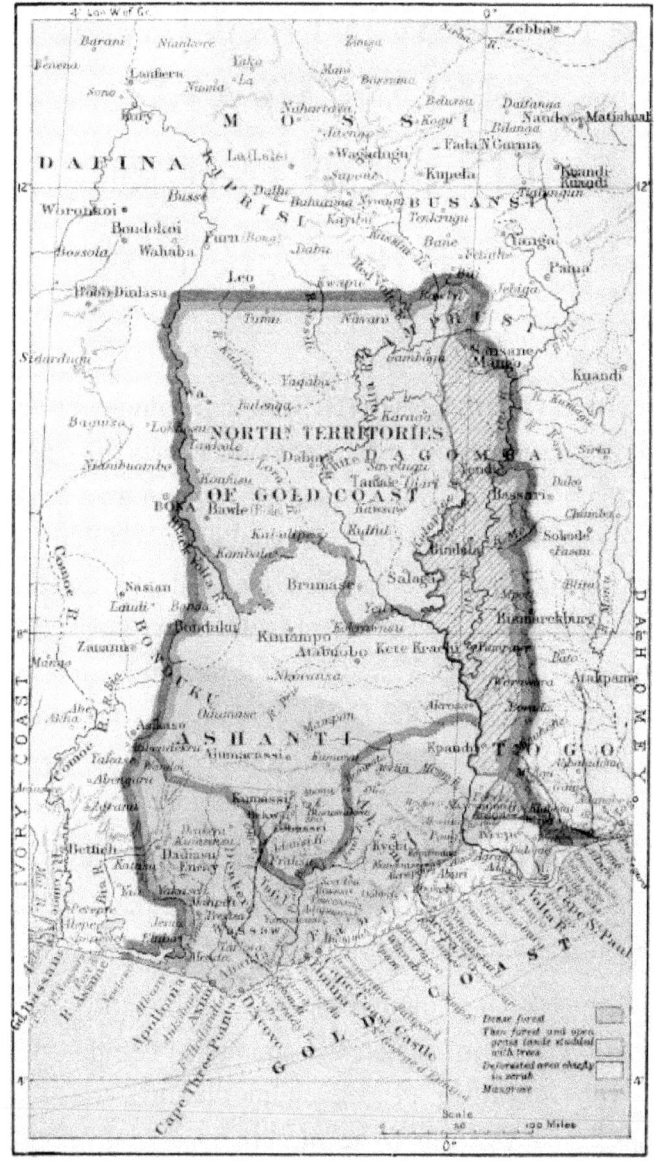

Stanford's Geogl. Estabt., London.

THE GOLD COAST, ASHANTI AND THE NORTHERN TERRITORIES

INTRODUCTORY REMARKS. Geographical Position.—The Gold Coast Colony, with the dependencies of Ashanti and the Northern Territories, forms a nearly oblong tract of country, bounded on the north by the 11th parallel of north latitude and the French Sudan, on the south by the Gulf of Guinea, on the east by Togoland, and on the west by the Ivory Coast (French). The course of the Black Volta forms the natural boundary on the north-west, and that of the Daka, continued as the main Volta river, a large extent of the eastern, which, however, is in course of realignment.

Area and Population.—The area of the whole country is estimated at about 82,000 sq. miles, and the population at upwards of 1,500,000.

Divisions.—The Colony proper forms the most southern of the three divisions of which the country is composed, and is bounded on the north by an irregular line dividing it from Ashanti. This line commences upon the western frontier at a point about 6° 40′ N. and 3° 7′ W., and runs to a point on the Ofin river about 6° 30′ N. and 2° W., continuing southward along the course of the Ofin to its junction with the Pra river, whence it follows the last-named river in a north-easterly direction to near Abetifi, and continues in an irregular line to the Volta, meeting it below the junction of the Assuokoko stream. Ashanti is separated from the Northern Territories by an irregular boundary-line from east to west, on the south side of the Black and main Volta rivers. It is almost entirely forested up to the boundaries of the largest towns. A view of Kumassi, the capital, is given, showing the proximity of the forest (Fig. 14).

From a climatic as well as an agricultural standpoint the country is more conveniently divided into two parts by a line which sharply defines the limits of the region of dense forest from that of the grass lands with few trees, which is characteristic of the country to the north. This line is probably the northern limit of the tract of country subject to a prolonged rainy season, and owing to the density of the forest south of it seems to have constituted the extreme distance to which the Mohammedan conquerors from the north were able to penetrate, when attempting to subdue and convert the pagan tribes to their south. The improved methods of agriculture found among the tribes inhabiting the ultra-forest country of the Northern Territories may be attributable to the teaching of these conquering people. On account of the marked differences in the conditions and the agricultural development of the forest and ultra-forest regions, it appears to be more convenient to refer to the products from the Northern Territories in a separate part, and this course has been followed here.

PART I.—GOLD COAST AND ASHANTI

Origin of Tribes.—Tradition among the natives maintains that the two great tribes of Fanti and Ashanti were originally from the same stock, and it is probable that this was also the case with regard to the people of Tufel, Denkera, Assin and Aquapim, who are said to speak a dialect of the same language as that of the Fantis and Ashantis. Completely different languages are, however, spoken by the Appolonias, Ahantas, Agoonahs, Accras, and Adampes living near the coast, and these are supposed to represent the remains of an earlier race.

The native belief is that the whole people were originally composed of twelve families or tribes, and that each was called by a separate name in some way indicating the occupation. According to Bowdich, those calling themselves after animals of the forest probably represented the families employing their time in hunting, and those bearing such names as cornstalk (Abrotoo) and plantain (Abbradi) applied themselves to agriculture. The name Agoonah, implying "oil-palm locality," seems to have been applied to all those who were traders. Individuals are still said to assume these distinctive names without regard to their usual tribal affinities.

The probable reason for the backward condition of agriculture in the forest region is that a food supply was procurable from the forest itself, and the continual intertribal warfare, in which the people seemed to have been engaged, was opposed to the cultivation of crops, which might become an incentive to a covetous attack. More recently, since these conditions have become altered, through the pacification of the country, some of the tribes, who were the first to become settled, have adopted a form of cultivation which, although wasteful, seems to be common among the forest people of West Africa. By means of imperfect clearing of the ground before cultivation, and superficial turning up of the soil, small crops of grain (maize) and roots (yams and cassava) are raised, and the land is usually left to revert to a state of weeds and "bush" after two or three years' use. This resembles the "Chena" system in Ceylon. The tribes who have developed a better and more economical form of working are those in whose districts the advent of cocoa planters has so raised the value of land that they are compelled to utilise the same plot more frequently for their annual crops. As an indication of this, the best cultivated fields are those of the Krobos, Akims, Krepes, and Kwahus, while the least advanced tribes are the Ashantis.

Owing to the remunerative return from cocoa cultivation in parts of the country, this commodity has attained the first place among exported agricultural and forest products. In recent years, moreover, development has been so rapid that the country is now the largest producer of cocoa in the world. Among exports, rubber, palm oil, palm kernels and timber follow it in order of importance.

COCOA.—As a preliminary to an account of the cocoa industry in the Gold Coast, it may be considered useful to refer briefly to the botanical position of the tree which produces cocoa, as well as to the varieties which are cultivated. A comparison of the methods employed in the Gold Coast with those adopted elsewhere seems also necessary.

The tree is a native of Trinidad and the north-eastern part of South America, and is botanically classified in the Natural Order *Sterculiaceæ*, sub-Order *Buettnerieæ*, under the name of *Theobroma cacao* of Linnæus.

In the West Indies, from which the cultivation has spread into several tropical countries, three fairly well-marked varieties are recognised as commercially useful, and these bear the local names of "Criollo," "Forastero," and "Calabacillo." The first of these is said to be identical with that occurring at Caracas, in Venezuela, and is usually called by the name of that place when exported from South America. The *Criollo* variety is the source of some of the highest-priced produce, but *Forastero* has some points in its favour for general cultivation, the chief of which appears to be greater hardiness. For this reason it seems to have become easily established in the islands of San Thomé and Fernando Po, where the sub-variety known as *Amelonado* is that of general occurrence, and to have spread from there to the mainland of West Africa. In Ceylon the *Forastero* variety is also much grown in plantations. The third variety, *Calabacillo*, yields an inferior product and does not appear to have been introduced into the eastern hemisphere.[1]

Cocoa, as shipped from the plantations, is the dried bean or seed, which has been removed from the fruit pod of the tree, and may or may not have been fermented before drying. The properly fermented seeds or beans find more favour in European markets than those which have not undergone the process, but it is chiefly in an imperfectly fermented condition that cocoa beans are exported from the Gold Coast. Attempts are being made to alter this, so as to produce a better quality.

Cocoa forms a very nutritious food, and beverage after preparation by the manufacturer, entering the markets in a manufactured form under the names of cocoa or chocolate. No native manufacture is employed in the Gold Coast, although cocoa butter has been extracted on a small scale at Odumase.

The following account is that which is generally accepted regarding the first introduction of the tree into the Gold Coast. About the year 1879 a native trader, named Tete Quasshi, brought some of the seed from Fernando Po and made a small plantation at Mampong, which is situated about ten miles north of Aburi in the Volta River District. The trees grew well, and the first crops of pods were said to have been disposed of to other natives at £1 per pod. Following the example of this trader, the Basel Mission Trading Association imported more pods from Fernando Po, and for some time they were able to dispose of them at a large profit. The variety introduced was *Forastero-Amelonado*, and was found to thrive extremely well under the local conditions prevalent in the districts of the Volta River, Kwahu, and Eastern Akim.

The first shipment of cocoa from the Gold Coast was made in 1891, when 80 lbs., valued at £4, were exported. From that time onward the annual exported quantity has increased somewhat irregularly until the returns for 1919 show 176,155 tons, worth more than £8,000,000.

No estimate can be given of the area at present under cocoa cultivation, for the reason that a large number of the cultivators only possess a few trees standing near their houses or scattered in their farms. Where plantations exist they are usually small, and, owing to the irregularity of the planting, no efficient idea of the possible production could be obtained by measurement of the planted area alone.

Since the settlement of the Ashantis into more peaceful modes of living, and the adoption by them of agricultural work, cocoa planting has rapidly spread through Ashanti-Akim, and new plantations may be found even westward of Kumassi. From

Axim also there is an extension of cocoa-growing towards the north, and it has recently been stated that the most promising land for the cultivation of the tree is to be found to the west of the railway, between Sekondi and Kumassi. The once proverbially truculent and warlike Ashantis have recently, to a large extent, become peaceful cocoa planters. Plantations are also found under European control, often in combination with rubber or kola; but cocoa does not combine with rubber as satisfactorily as coffee, which is more frequently employed. Under "Rubber" some particulars of the plantations, whose returns are available, are supplied.

In common with many other cultivated plants, cocoa requires certain definite combinations of climate and soil to ensure remunerative cultivation, and unless these exist the introduction is not to be recommended. With regard to climate, a considerable rainfall is generally thought necessary, the intervals of dry weather not being too prolonged. The drainage of the land should be good, for if the water cannot drain away within a reasonably short time, the trees will be adversely and often severely affected. Although it is recognised that cocoa can sustain itself under conditions of drought for a short time, districts subject to periodical absence of rain for a month or more are unsuitable, and trees planted in such places will generally die after a brief period. The annual rainfall in the cocoa districts of Trinidad averages about 72 inches, but a much heavier fall is experienced in the plantations of Ceylon. In neither of these countries, however, is there an annual long period of complete drought, which is a feature common in most parts of West Africa; and even when an interval without rain occurs, the humidity of the atmosphere compensates for the absence of it. Ceylon is visited by a double monsoon or rainy season, which is also the case in a less marked degree in the Gold Coast. The next requirement of importance is a soil of suitable quality. It is generally considered best to select land which possesses a moderate amount of loose clay mixed with sand, and, if the surface be thickly covered with vegetable deposit, so much the better. Steep hillsides, stiff, boggy, sandy, or rocky land are to be avoided. The presence of low scrub on uncleared land is an indication of poverty of soil, although the presence of heavy forest does not necessarily guarantee the suitability of the locality, as imperfectly drained land often bears a heavy forest growth. Good natural drainage is essential, and is nearly always found where the land slopes and the rock underlying the soil is friable or deep. Natural drainage can often be improved by artificial means. The last important condition necessary is the selection of a position where shade and wind protection can be obtained naturally to as great an extent as possible. Plantations in valleys, sheltered by mountain spurs or by belts of high forest, are suitable, and such formations are met with in many parts of the Gold Coast and Ashanti. In these localities the climate as well as the positions and soil obtainable are generally so well adapted for the fruitful growth of cocoa that, even where the average annual rainfall is as low as 41 inches (the average at Aburi), plantations are proving successful, the regular distribution, humidity of the atmosphere, and the natural shade constituting a compensation for the shortage.

The native planter sows the seeds in small patches or in roughly prepared beds in the vicinity of water, often in such proximity to one another as to choke a number of the young plants. This form of nursery is met with throughout the forests, and it is common to find circular patches containing two or three hundred plants adjoining a road. In addition to this, a large number of seedlings are grown at, and distributed from, the Government Botanic Gardens. Native plantations are for the most part formed of irregular lines of trees, generally planted too closely. The evil effect of this does not become apparent until the trees attain a large size, when the excessive shade they afford to their fruit-bearing branches, which in cocoa consist of the trunk and main structure, prevents the fruit from forming and induces rot through want of evaporation of moisture. The native planter is slow to recognise this, and disinclined to remedy the matter by removing some of the trees. The distance at which cocoa trees are planted by the native is roughly from 7 to 10 feet apart, whereas that recommended for plantations in the West Indies and Ceylon varies, with the quality of the soil and the elevation, from 12 to 15 feet; the latter would be more suitable for most of the Gold Coast plantations. The advantage which the native planter sees in his method of planting is, that in addition to getting a larger number of trees into a given space, the density of their foliage soon becomes so great that weeds cease to grow beneath, rendering cultivation unnecessary. Until such a state has been arrived at, the cutting of weeds is an operation which may have to be performed twice, or even three times, in the year. This is the only form of cultivation given, no manure being used or any breaking of the soil done. In the West Indies it is not customary to disturb the surface soil, except in so far as it may be necessary to apply manure or remove catch crops; but even in these cases great care is exercised, as it is found that the cocoa tree is to a large extent a surface feeder, and spreads lateral fine roots at very little depth below the surface. Shade is obtained naturally to a large degree, but in the early years of the tree's existence, cassava and plantains are planted to afford it. The plantation of Para rubber with cocoa has been recommended in such a manner that each would occur alternately in a diagonal line. This does not appear a very satisfactory plan, owing to the fact that Para rubber trees in West Africa shed their leaves annually at about the time that cocoa most needs shade. In the small patches of cocoa trees, which constitute most of the native plantations, permanent and sufficient shade is generally given by the surrounding forest trees, and it is of small importance in such cases to consider the plantation of permanent shade trees.

Pruning, in the West Indies, is attended with the greatest amount of care, and is performed for the purpose of producing a vigorous tree by the removal of all useless wood, and of encouraging fruiting branches to increase their production. In order to do the latter it is essential to remove any superfluous number of primary branches, three or four being considered sufficient for one tree. A similar regulation of growth is required with regard to the secondary and tertiary branches. In addition to this, care is given to retain the correct balance for the tree, and, when cutting out branches, to avoid making jagged cuts or slashes. The West African native does not prune with these objects in view, but employs a "cutlass" or "machete" to cut out those branches which seem to be giving too much shade or which have become interlaced, regardless of their value to the tree or of the wounds inflicted in the operation. Efforts have been made to teach pruning at the Botanical Stations, but the demonstrations have not been largely attended, and a great deal of damage continues to be done through ignorance of the objects and effects of pruning. Many of the older plantations, owing to bad treatment and too close planting, are yielding an annually diminishing crop, but new ones are springing up in increasing numbers each year, which is an obvious indication that the industry is proving a profitable one.

Insect Pests and Vegetable Parasites.—Wounds, such as those described above, often render the tree more susceptible to the attacks of insect pests; but, although it has been stated that cocoa trees in the Gold Coast are seriously affected in this way, such is not often the case. Beetles of the *Longicorn* group are found damaging the tree to some extent wherever it has been planted. Two species are recorded from the West Indies: *Steirastoma histrionica*, White, from Trinidad, and *S. depressa*, Linn., from Grenada. On the trees in the Gold Coast *Armatosterna buquetiana*, White, and a *Glenea sp.* have been found doing similar damage. These insects deposit their eggs in crevices of the bark or on wounds, and the grubs which emerge bore into the trunk, living and growing in size in the interior of the wood until mature, when they change into pupæ, and finally into beetles. The presence of these grubs is easily detected by the quantity of fine particles of wood or "frass" which are thrown out of the entrance hole; and, if a flexible wire be inserted until it reaches and impales the grub, it will often prevent the damage becoming serious. The nests of large red ants (*Œcophylla sp.*), which feed upon the saccharine juices which exude from the pods, may often be observed on cocoa trees, but as the ants viciously bite any living thing which may venture upon the tree, they are probably a safeguard against the depredations of rats and squirrels that eat out the contents of the ripe fruit while still on the tree.

COCOA AT MRAMRA ATTACKED BY BLACK COCOA-BARK BUG.
Fig. 16

DRYING COCOA BEANS AT MRAMRA.
Fig. 17

NATIVE TAPPING INDIGENOUS RUBBER TREE (*FUNTUMIA ELASTICA*), OBOAMANG, ASHANTI.

Fig. 18

In 1909 the writer drew attention to a black hemipterous insect causing destruction to plantations in the Ashanti-Akim region, where careless cultivation prevailed (cf. *Bull. Entom. Research*, vol. i. pt. viii. 1910). This insect, known as the "Black cocoa-bark bug" or "Sankonuabe," was named *Sahlbergella theobroma*, Distant, and subsists in all its stages upon the sap of cocoa branches obtained through punctures made by its proboscis.[2] The attacked trees are atrophied or killed outright (Fig. 16). Spraying with petroleum-soap emulsion has proved an effective remedy, but native planters do not readily adopt it. Recently the insect has been found sapping the silk cotton tree, and planters are warned against having this tree in their plantations.

Another insect, which belongs to the same Order as the last, and the genus *Helopeltis*, has been observed puncturing the pods and causing them to become black-spotted, distorted, and sometimes killed by the attack. This is allied to *H. Antonii*, Sign., which punctures cocoa pods in the same manner in Ceylon. The insect does not appear to be numerous at present, but should be sought on damaged pods and killed at every opportunity, as some species of the same genus have developed into the worst enemies of tea and cinchona in other parts of the world.

Fungoid parasites appear to be rare in the Gold Coast, although they have been observed commonly in other places in Africa. In some of the damper parts of Ashanti a fungoid thread blight was observed on cocoa, and was found to be common upon several forest shrubs in the same places. This is perhaps *Stilbum nanum*, Massee; it should be treated by means of scraping with a wooden knife combined with spraying with Bordeaux mixture.

Harvesting and Preparing.—The native cocoa grower

collects the pods from his trees at the time when he estimates he can gather the most, and, in consequence, many over-ripe and under-ripe fruits are taken with the ripe. The effect of this is to give an irregular product which can never possess the attributes of a good cocoa. The pods are usually pulled off the tree, a knife being seldom used; and in the action of pulling off, the cushion, upon which the pod is borne, is often torn and injured. As it is from this point, or near it, that the successive crops of flowers and fruits proceed, the bearing power of the tree is frequently diminished in this way. The use of a knife and the necessity for frequent pickings, to ensure the pods being taken when mature, are among the most important lessons which the native planter should be taught. The pods after collection are thrown into a heap upon the ground, and are often left without further attention for two or three days, after which they are broken open with the aid of a "cutlass," and the contents are scooped out into a basket. The result is a mixture of beans, in their surrounding pulp, in different stages of maturity. The length of time that the beans remain in the basket is generally only regulated by the convenience of the collector. The next operation is to remove as much of the pulp as possible by washing in a stream, and this is more easily effected with the over-ripe beans or with those which have been allowed to "sweat" or ferment. After washing, the beans are spread thinly upon mats, raised upon rough frames, in order to dry them in the sun. An illustration is given showing this process (Fig. 17). Such is the crude and irregular method employed by the natives of the Gold Coast, who until quite recently had little or no knowledge of the advantages of fermentation. Owing to the small quantities with which they worked at one time, it is probable that the fermenting action in the pulp was seldom set up. During the last few years attention has been given to this by the more intelligent planters, and it is not uncommon to find that boxes and barrels have been brought into use by them, and that fermentation has been allowed to proceed for from four to ten days with satisfactory results. Drying is still conducted in the manner described above, and is often incomplete, but, to remedy the defects of this, one of the European buying firms has erected a drying machine, in which all the cocoa bought is thoroughly dried before shipment.

The skilled cocoa planter of the West Indies and Ceylon is careful to pick only those pods which are quite mature, and, in order to do this, he is obliged to go over his plantation frequently. Mature pods are those which have assumed a yellowish or reddish colour, and considerable experience is necessary to judge this with accuracy. The pods are removed by means of a cutting instrument called a "cocoa hook," with which care can be more easily given to the preservation of the cushion. The pods are placed in heaps and, in the case of small estates where one day's picking is insufficient to procure a fermentation, they are left for, perhaps, two days until a sufficient quantity has been obtained. Sorting, according to variety and degree of maturity, is resorted to before opening, and, again, when cut open, care is taken to separate such beans as are found over-ripe. This practice is strictly adhered to in Ceylon, but is often disregarded in the West Indies. No washing is done at this stage, but the beans, with their pulp attached, are placed in barrels, boxes, or vats for the purpose of fermentation, which is brought about by the decomposition of the pulp, and is complete when the liquor, thus formed, has impregnated the interior of the bean and changed the colour of it from purple to rich chocolate brown. The shell becomes toughened, and the remaining pulp is more easily removed after this process has been undergone. Washing, if it is considered necessary, is then proceeded with, and is generally done in Ceylon, though not in the West Indies. Drying is chiefly done in the sun in the West Indies, and the beans are spread thickly and turned constantly. Drying houses, which have roofs capable of being slid over the cocoa on the approach of rain, are used. In Ceylon hot air distributed by centrifugal fans is the common method. Polishing, which is often employed in the West Indies, is done by sifting finely powdered red earth over the partly dried beans while they are exposed to the sun, when, it is maintained, the earth assists to remove the remaining pulp as well as to absorb the moisture, at the same time giving the surfaces of the beans a polished exterior. Annatto is said to be used instead of red earth in Venezuela, but the addition of this is, presumably, with the object of colouring, rather than polishing. "Dancing" is an operation designed to prevent the development of mildew, and consists of treading the beans with the bare feet.

Some of the large manufacturers in Europe have recommended that the Gold Coast planters should ferment their produce, but should not wash the beans after fermentation.

Markets.—Certain large cocoa-buying centres are recognised, which, in the Volta River district, are situated at the foot of the hilly country, in positions convenient for transport to the ports of shipment. In addition to these, however, a good deal of buying is proceeded with at smaller places in the midst of the growing districts, but these probably represent the localities for the transactions carried on by agents or middlemen. Until the produce is actually in the hands of the shippers, the conveyance of cocoa is almost entirely done by head-loads of about 60 lbs. The head-load is the standard for trading, and the local price quoted is always with reference to it. It is customary for the buying shippers to send out their agents to the cocoa districts to arrange for the purchase of the crops, and it is always necessary that such purchases should be paid for in silver, no notes or cheques being accepted. Owing to competition during the past few years, the agents have often paid the grower a sum of money long before his crop was ready for picking, in order to guarantee that it may be bought by no one else. This has had the effect of making the grower careless in the preparation of his crop, and has caused the production of much bad material. The report that at another town, often distant by many days' journey, a higher price is being paid than that obtained in a market close at hand, will frequently induce a native to convey his head-loads to the distant market, regardless of the fact that the extra shilling or so he may receive does not appear to be sufficient compensation for the additional labour and time expended. This points to the fact that the native does not put the same value on his time and labour when he is working for himself as he does when he is employed by others.

The buyers of cocoa pack it in bags for shipment, and these are conveyed to the ports by motor lorries or placed inside large casks, similar to those used for palm oil, and rolled along the roads. Some of the shipments are conveyed in river steamers on the Volta, and, more recently, owing to the growers having found a better market for a short time at Kumassi, a considerable amount was sent by rail from that place to Sekondi. In consequence of the imperfect state of dryness in which the cocoa is often sold by the planter, a great amount of care should be exercised before mixing and packing. Sorting is not much practised, and some of the beans often become attacked by mildew before reaching Europe, which depreciates the value of the whole package. It is partly owing to the disregard of the precautions of sorting and final drying that the West African cocoa has earned such a bad name, and if more shippers were to follow the example set by the one firm that has erected a drying apparatus, it would do much to improve matters in this direction. Cocoa is difficult to dry completely in the growing districts by means of the sun, as the atmosphere in these localities is often so humid that the beans absorb moisture when removed from the sun's rays, and it is for this reason especially that the final drying should be done by the shippers. Transport to the ports of shipment from the growing districts will be facilitated by the construction of a short railway, which it is contemplated making from Accra, and until this is ready the carriage by head-loads, cask-rolling, and motor lorries will probably continue. The presence of the "tsetse" fly throughout the growing districts prevents the possibility of draught cattle being used.

A system of pooling purchases was agreed upon some years ago by a number of leading shippers, in accordance with which competition among themselves was suppressed, and a fixed price was to be given for all cocoa. This action was doubtless taken in order to prevent ruinous competition, but had the effect of checking improvement in the quality, as no encouragement was given to the planter to prepare the cocoa with greater care. The few shippers who did not join in this "combine" were enabled to obtain the better qualities at a very slightly enhanced price. In 1906 the general quality of Gold Coast cocoa had so deteriorated that the merchants were asked by the Government for their assistance to improve it. This led to an inquiry which revealed the state of affairs mentioned above. The obvious remedy of paying a price according to quality did not find favour with the combine, who appear to have argued that it would not profit them to pay a higher price for the small variable lots of improved produce which might result. It was stated by some of the local merchants in Accra that Gold Coast cocoa was generally suitable for sale in certain European markets, where it was adapted for the manufacture of a cheap form of sweetmeat, and that, if the quality were improved and the price raised in consequence, damage would be done to a new and rapidly growing trade. The merchants ultimately agreed to endeavour to improve the standard of quality, and it was arranged that all the cocoa brought in to the markets at Aimensa and Dodowa should be graded, with a view to regulating the price according to grade. This plan fell through at the last moment, as a test sample of picked cocoa was said to have been priced at only 1*s.* 6*d.* per cwt. over ordinary "Accra" in the European market. The fall in the value of the residue was said to be uncompensated for by the small increase mentioned.

Improvement of Quality.—Inquiries conducted by the Imperial Institute pointed to the fact that well-prepared Gold Coast cocoa could obtain high prices in Europe. In 1907 a consignment was sent to the Imperial Institute for examination and report, and proved to be of good quality, and when subsequently sold, it obtained a high price. This established confidence with regard to the possibility of fine grades being prepared in the country. During this year, owing to the action of the Fernando Po and San Thomé growers, in withholding their crop, a greater demand was created for Gold Coast cocoa, and the advent of large buyers, working outside the "combine," forced the local price to a high figure. This did not assist in the improvement of the quality, as the competition induced native buying agents to buy the produce in almost any form, in consequence of which large quantities of imperfectly dried stuff were obtained. On the market becoming steadier, many of the more intelligent natives realised the advantage of careful preparation, to which they are now turning their attention.

Towards this latter result Messrs. Cadbury Bros., Ltd., rendered great assistance. This firm sent representatives into the country, who proved to the natives that they were willing to pay an enhanced price for cocoa prepared in a manner suitable for their requirements. A fair amount of cocoa was purchased by them, and demonstrations were made in some places with regard to the proper mode of fermentation. In addition to this a number of seedlings of the *Criollo* variety were given to the Agricultural Department for experimental work at the Aburi Botanic Station.

The *Forastero-amelonado* variety, a hardy but commercially inferior kind, has been mainly employed in plantations, and experiments have been carried on for some years at Aburi with *Pentagona, Caracas* and *Cundeamor* besides *Criollo* mentioned above. Such good results were obtained with *Cundeamor* that, in 1913, keen competition was aroused among planters to obtain seed. The years 1913 and 1914 are said to have shown an improvement in the quality of the cocoa produced. The attention of the Agricultural Department has been given to the general instruction of the natives in improved methods of cultivation and preparation, both by means of lectures and demonstrations at the Botanic Stations and by the issue of pamphlets in English and the Twi language. There was at first an insufficient staff for instruction to be given except at the Botanic Stations, and only those growers who lived in the vicinity were able to obtain benefit from it. After holding several conferences with chiefs and planters in the cocoa districts it became evident that the appointment of European Travelling Instructors was necessary, and following this the Government detailed certain officers for the work; the object being that they should occupy a large portion of their time in travelling through the country in order to give personal instruction to the natives in correct methods of treating cocoa and other agricultural products. Persons selected by chiefs are now trained to act as instructors in planting in their own native towns.

The preparation of a large quantity of cocoa of even quality is so greatly dependent upon the similarity of the treatment and conditions at a time when the material is undergoing fermentation and drying, that it is almost imperative that a large quantity should be prepared at one operation. This is an important consideration in British West Africa, where native plantations range in size from a few trees to about five acres in extent, the average being perhaps about a hundred trees, or, roughly, one-tenth of an acre. The production of each plantation is at present prepared independently, and the result of one picking of pods, if all mature, is often quite inadequate to yield sufficient for fermentation purposes, it being recognised that a few hundredweights of beans in their pulp are necessary for the satisfactory accomplishment of the operation. The same difficulty has presented itself in the West Indies with regard to the crops picked by owners of small plantations, and arrangements are usually made by some larger concern in the neighbourhood to purchase the pods from them. The establishment of central fermenting and drying houses, controlled by the shippers themselves, would perhaps get over the difficulty on the Gold Coast and result in a superior class of cocoa being produced. The planters would doubtless consent to sell their pods, instead of performing the laborious work of preparation themselves, and would probably be able to extend the size of their individual plantations, which, by reason of their inability to prepare more cocoa, single-handed, they have been unable, hitherto, to do. The efforts of the Administration to improve the preparation have been somewhat handicapped by the system employed by some merchants of securing the crop for themselves, by money advances, with but little regard to its preparation, and of pooling the produce.

Cocoa planting has revolutionised the native system of land titles. Where only annual crops were under consideration, a short, temporary occupation with subsequent reversion to tribal ownership seemed an adequate provision, but with the establishment of permanent cocoa plantations the planter claimed perpetual and undivided proprietorship.

Further information regarding Gold Coast cocoa will be found in the *Bulletin of the Imperial Institute*, 1907, p. 361; 1912, pp. 240, 556; 1913, p. 154; 1914, p. 387; 1915, pp. 149, 645; 1916, p. 123; 1917, p. 117; 1919, pp. 49, 102; and Johnson's *Cocoa*, 1912.

Exports of Cocoa.—The exports of cocoa from 1900 to 1919 are as follows:

Year	Tons	Year	Tons	Year	Tons
1900	536	1907	9,355	1914	52,888
1901	980	1908	12,743	1915	77,278
1902	2,396	1909	20,213	1916	72,162
1903	2,276	1910	22,631	1917	90,964
1904	5,112	1911	39,726	1918	66,342
1905	5,093	1912	38,647	1919	176,155
1906	8,975	1913	50,554		

RUBBER. Indigenous Species.—The most important source of rubber in the Gold Coast and Ashanti is the indigenous tree locally called "Ofruntum"; a comparatively small amount is also derived from some of the vines belonging to the same Natural Order, and from one or more of the wild trees of the Ficus Order.

Reports on the quality and commercial value of some of the principal kinds of rubber obtained in the Gold Coast are published in the *Bulletin of the Imperial Institute*, vol. v. (1907), p. 248.

Botanical Position of the "Ofruntum" Tree.—The "Ofruntum," or African rubber, is botanically placed in the Natural Order *Apocynaceæ*, under the specific name of *Funtumia elastica*, Stapf. Until recently it was referred to as *Kicksia africana*, Benth. and others (a genus which is not known to occur in West Africa), and it was also confused with a very nearly allied species, occurring in the same localities, and now known as *Funtumia africana*, Stapf. Owing to the great similarity which these species of Funtumia bear to one another, it is important that the differences between them should be recognised, *F. africana* not furnishing any but very inferior rubber. The most reliable method of testing the species which produces rubber, is by rubbing a small quantity of latex between the finger and thumb, when small particles of rubber should be quickly formed, the latex of *F. africana* becoming only a sticky mass under the operation. The leaf of *F. elastica* can usually be recognised by the presence of a small pit at the origin of each secondary nerve or vein on the under-surface, which feature is not characteristic of the leaf of *F. africana*, although recently individual trees have been found exhibiting this peculiarity. The flower bud of *F. elastica* is typically much shorter than that of *F. africana*, and the double seed pod of the former species is shorter and more blunt than that of the latter.

Distribution of *F. elastica*.—The Funtumia rubber tree occurs in a wild state in the forests throughout the Gold Coast and Ashanti, although it has been nearly exterminated in some parts. It appears to be most plentiful in the dense forest regions of Northern Ashanti.

Native Methods for Preparing.—Funtumia rubber is exported under the names of "Ashanti lump" and "Niggers," which consist of much adulterated, evil-smelling substances, for which a low price is procurable in comparison with that paid for pure rubber. In certain years the demand for this has been maintained, but the adequate supplies of good rubber from elsewhere, and the rapid expansion of the cocoa industry, have caused a diminution in the export of native-made rubber, which has been replaced to a small extent by plantation rubber.

The wild trees grow from 50 to 100 feet in height, and often have a girth of three feet at four feet from the base; the trunk being commonly without branches for a considerable height. The native ascends the trunk by means of a sling passed round it, to one end of which is a loop which fits over his right thigh and to the other a stirrup in which he keeps his left foot. By moving the rope up the tree the ascent is quickly accomplished, and when stationary, both hands are left free. The climber carries a gouge, or semi-cylindrically-faced chisel, with which he cuts vertical as well as transverse oblique grooves, forming a rough "herring-bone" pattern, which may be continued for the whole length of the trunk, and even extend on to the main branches. To make the cuts the tool is either used in one hand or is held in the left and driven by blows on the end of the handle, given with the palm of the right hand. The flow of latex commences at once, and is directed down the vertical channel into a calabash placed at the base of the tree, into which the latex is guided by a lip of clay or a chip of wood. The illustration shows a native in Ashanti tapping a tree (Fig. 18). The quantity of latex procured at the one tapping varies; an exceptionally large amount being about two quarts from a large tree. The tree is not tapped again for several months and until the wounds have healed. On the second tapping the same form of cuts is made upon the opposite side of the tree, and the transverse channels often intersect those made previously; besides this, owing to the want of regulation in the depth of the cuts, the inner or cambium layer of the bark may be so damaged that the intersecting cuts may ring the tree and cause death. Few trees probably survive the third or fourth tapping.

"ODUM" TREES CHLOROPHORA EXCELSA.
Fig. 19

PARA RUBBER TREE (*HEVEA BRASILIENSIS*), TAPPED AT ABURI.
Fig. 20

RUBBER TREE TAPPED, HERRING-BONE SYSTEM IMPERFECT, ABURI. Fig. 21

If the herring-bone cuts were made carefully upon the lower part of the trunk, and attention given to their depth and direction, the tree might be preserved for a longer period. An illustration given shows the incorrect mode of tapping, where the transverse cuts are opposite instead of alternate (Fig. 21). Experiments seem to show that there is not the same "wound response" in the case of Funtumia trees as is found in that of the "Para" tree (*Hevea brasiliensis*); the paring of the wounds some days after tapping yielding no flow of latex similar to that procured in the first instance. On cutting the bark area between the transverse channels, the latex cells appeared to be empty and to indicate that a large area is drained on the first tapping. Further investigation is necessary in order to compare the results obtained from this tree with those of *Hevea*.

The latex of Funtumia will remain in an uncoagulated state for a longer time than that of Hevea, but it may become damaged by fermentation if a quantity is kept in bulk for a lengthened period. The native does not usually produce a pure Funtumia rubber, but mixes with the latex the latices of several other plants, among which may be named "Odum" (*Chlorophora excelsa*), "Osese" (*Funtumia africana*), "Ofo," "Okre," "Sindru" (*Conopharyngia crassa* and *Alstonia sp.*). Having mixed some of these latices with that of the Funtumia, the whole is heated and poured into a hole in the ground, which has been prepared to serve as a mould. Coagulation and decomposition proceed together at a slow rate, and finally produce a rubber containing a number of holes which serve as receptacles for the liquefied decomposed constituents. The rubber mass is black outwardly, but whitish within, and is more or less sticky. It is said that the latex of *Landolphia owariensis*, the vine from which "Krepi ball" rubber is made, is sometimes mixed with the rest to hasten coagulation.

Improved Methods.—In 1906 attention was drawn to the use of a plant called "Niama" in the Ivory Coast, by which Funtumia rubber latex was coagulated by adding a hot decoction of the leaves. This plant was subsequently found to be *Bauhinia reticulata*, which bears the name of "Otakataka" in the Gold Coast. Experiments with this afforded excellent results. An examination of the plant made at the Imperial Institute proved that the tannin contained in the leaves was responsible for the coagulation of the latex, and that the infusion of any plant containing tannin is equally effective. The obstacle to the general use of *B. reticulata* for coagulation, is that the plant does not occur in the same localities as the wild Funtumia tree. Doubtless other tannin-yielding plants may be found in the rubber forests which would answer the purpose equally well, among them the pods of *Acacia arabica*. A simple method of coagulation, which was demonstrated to the chiefs and rubber collectors in 1908, is that of diluting the latex with about four or more times the volume of water, straining and boiling it, when the rubber quickly separates and can be collected from the surface of the water by means of a stick and immediately pressed into a rough biscuit.

The rubber made in the manner mentioned above has been valued at more than twice the price obtained for the adulterated stuff, but it appears difficult to persuade the local merchants to offer a higher price for it, and it therefore suits the rubber collector better to make the inferior quality. So long as this state of things continues, it is to be feared that instruction in the improvement of quality will not lead to the adoption of better methods.

In 1908 a Commission of Enquiry was appointed and made certain recommendations for legislation for the protection of the industry. Articles on Gold Coast rubber will be found in the *Bulletin of the Imperial Institute*, vols. viii. (1910), x. (1912), xi. (1913), xii. (1914), xii. (1915) and xv. (1917).

Plantations.—Large numbers of Funtumia seedlings have been grown at and distributed from the Government Botanic Gardens at Aburi, Tarkwa, and Kumassi, and some of the Ashanti kings and chiefs, who have expressed a wish to attempt to renovate their rubber forests, have obtained assistance from the officers of the Agricultural Department, who have conducted planting operations in the forests in the presence of those interested. Plantations under European management and with European capital are in progress in the vicinity of Axim and Sekondi. Most of the recently made plantations are said to consist more of Para than of Funtumia rubber trees, although in 1913 one of these in the Dunkwa district of Ashanti was reported to contain 20,000 trees of the latter kind. The tree appears to thrive well when planted closely, and straight trunks are soon formed.

Insect Pest.—At Aburi and elsewhere the Funtumia tree is found to be attacked by the larva of a moth of the family *Pyralidæ*, identified as *Glyphodes ocellata*, Hampson, which denudes it of leaves. No severe damage seems to be done by this pest, which has only been observed in plantations, and was destroyed at Aburi by repeated applications of lime and ashes.

Fungoid Pest.—A sooty fungoid growth is sometimes seen upon the leaves, similar to that occurring on orange trees in the country, and probably belongs to the genus *Meliola*. It is destroyed by the application of sprays of Bordeaux mixture.

Rubber Machinery.—A fully equipped installation of rubber-washing and crêpeing machinery was exhibited at the

Kumassi Agricultural Exhibition of 1908, and was subsequently taken over by one of the leading mercantile firms at that place, where the local rubber is now washed, crêped, and pressed before export. It might prove advantageous to come to an arrangement with the rubber collectors to bring the latex to Kumassi, where, under proper supervision, it could be made into rubber of high quality. As the latex will remain for a considerable time without alteration, it should not be difficult to bring it in from places several days' journey distant.

Vine Rubber.—Several species of vines, belonging to the Natural Order *Apocynaceæ*, produce rubber in Africa, but the only one of commercial importance occurring in the Gold Coast is *Landolphia owariensis*, Pal. Beauv., from which "Krepi" or "White ball" is obtained. Unless the plant is observed during the flowering as well as the fruiting season, it is difficult to distinguish it from some nearly allied, but useless, species of the same genus, which are found commonly in the same localities.

The vine is found throughout the forest region of the Gold Coast and Ashanti, climbing over and interlacing the main branches of large forest trees; but an apparently terrestrial form of the same species has recently been discovered in the ultra-forest region, where the stunted habit in which it grows is probably occasioned by the annual grass fires.

Under different atmospheric conditions the latex of *L. owariensis* behaves differently. In the drier regions it coagulates upon the wound almost immediately upon exposure to the air, whereas in other and moister places it runs from the cut in such a manner as to allow it to be collected in a vessel. The acid juices of some of the local wild fruits are added to hasten coagulation, when this is necessary, or the collector is said to smear the fresh latex upon his naked body, until enough has been coagulated to form a small ball, which serves as a nucleus for winding on the strings of fresh latex as the new cuts are made. There is a quantity of "scrap rubber" formed on the wedge-shaped cuts which it is usual to make, and this is added to the ball, which attains a diameter of three or four inches when complete. The crushing of the root and stem for the manufacture of so-called "root-rubber" does not appear to be practised in this country, although common elsewhere in West Africa.

On account of the colour and form of this rubber, the name of "White ball" is usually applied to it, although, from the fact that the Krepi tribes, living on the east bank of the Volta river, produce a large quantity of it, the name of "Krepi ball" is frequently given.

White ball rubber is seldom adulterated by the addition of other latices, as these would retard coagulation and interfere with the preparation of it in the manner mentioned. For this reason the rubber sold under this name usually obtains a higher price than other rubber.

Landolphia owariensis presents many disadvantages for cultivation in plantations, and the yield is small in proportion to the space which the plant occupies. Several species of this and allied genera are being grown experimentally at the Aburi Botanic Gardens.

"Flake rubber" is a name given to a very inferior quality of rubber which is produced upon a small scale in many parts of West Africa, but it has not been determined from which species of vine that exported from the Gold Coast is obtained. In Northern Nigeria *Carpodinus hirsutus*, Hua, is said to be the source of the exported rubber of this name.

Fig Rubber.—One or more species of wild fig trees (*Ficus sp.*) are tapped for the production of what is locally termed "Memeluku" rubber, and it is generally supposed that *F. Vogelii* is that mostly employed. The trees attain a large size, and the rubber is composed of the scrap, collected from a large number of small cuts made on the trunk and branches. This scrap rubber is pressed together into thick biscuits. The rubber has usually little resiliency and breaks easily; it is, in consequence, of small value.

Introduced Species.—Experiments have been carried on for several years with "Para" rubber (*Hevea brasiliensis*), "Ceara" (*Manihot Glaziovii*), and *Castilloa elastica*, all indigenous to South America. The last-named has been so badly attacked in the Botanic Stations by boring beetle larvæ that it has shown no promise of success. Ceara grows well, but for some reason the production of latex from it is uncertain, and this has caused little value to be attached to it in the Gold Coast, although in the drier region of Togoland this species is being planted. Para rubber seems to show much better results, although, up to the present, no extensive experiments to ascertain the yield of rubber have been made. Tapping two trees growing at Aburi, Mr. Johnson obtained a larger quantity of latex than from *Funtumia elastica* under the same conditions; and following this an extensive area was planted with Hevea trees at the Tarkwa Botanic Gardens, where the experiment appears to be proving successful. Views are given of a tree at Aburi (Fig. 20). Large plantations of Hevea are being made near Tarkwa, Axim and Sekondi as well as in the Kwahu district, where the tree seems to thrive remarkably well. A few of these plantations made returns in 1913 showing promise of success. At one, on the Offin river, there were said to be 90,000 Para trees of different ages, 20,000 Funtumia and

6,000 coffee (*C. robusta*). At another the yield of rubber from a number of mature trees gave an average of 1·08 lb. of dry rubber per tree in eight months' tapping, and a third had 22,000 Para trees of which about 8,450 had been tapped and yielded 10,565 lbs. of rubber, or 1¼ lb. per tree tapped. Labour was reported plentiful and good. There are said to be many more rubber plantations in the country from which returns had not been received. Up to 1913 the Agricultural Department had distributed 250,000 Para seedlings and 1,500,000 seeds.

Commenting on the fluctuation in the exported amounts of rubber, His Excellency the Governor (Sir Hugh Clifford), in his message to the Legislative Council in October 1918, explained the recrudescence during 1916 and 1917 as due to the development of rubber plantations under European control. It remains to be seen whether the Gold Coast will be able to successfully compete in this work with the Far East. Articles on Para rubber from the Gold Coast are to be found in the *Bulletin of the Imperial Institute*, vol. x. (1912), vol. xi. (1913), vol. xii. (1914), vol. xv. (1917) and vol. xvii. (1919).

PALM OIL AND KERNELS.—Records are available showing that the export of palm oil from West Africa has continued for over one hundred years, but the quantity shipped from the Gold Coast during the last fifteen years shows a rapid decrease from the average of the twenty years previous.

The tree which yields the oil of commerce is known as *Elæis guineensis*, Jacq., and is placed in the Tribe *Cocoineæ* of the Natural Order *Palmæ*, together with the genus *Cocos*, to which the Coconut palm belongs. (Cf. *Bull. Imp. Inst.*, 1909, p. 357; 1920, p. 209.)

Habits of the Oil Palm.—The oil palm occurs most

plentifully in the moist regions near the coast, although it will not thrive on land which is perpetually marshy. The palm becomes scarcer when the dense forests of Ashanti are reached, but it is not entirely absent until the ultra-forest tract commences.

The tree often bears fruit when it has only attained the height of ten feet, which it is said to do about the seventh year, but the yield is supposed to increase annually until the tree is thirty or more years old, often continuing for a much longer time. It is not possible to give any positive assurance on this point, as observations have not been recorded for any length of time.

Although the oil is principally obtained from wild trees, one extensive plantation in the Krobo Hills has been successfully carried on for many years by the chief of Odumassi. His trees are planted at regular intervals and care is given to their upkeep and cleanliness. Concessions have recently been granted to Europeans for planting as well as exploiting the wild palms, and experimental work in the mechanical extraction of pericarp and kernel oil have given some promise. Two British companies that have erected extraction plants in the Western Province have laid tram-lines designed to keep them constantly supplied with the palm fruit.

Trees that have become old and practically barren are usually tapped for the extraction of "palm wine," being frequently cut down for the purpose. In some parts of the country fruitful trees are tapped while standing, and, as this necessitates the base of the terminal shoot being cut into, the tree is generally killed in consequence.

Two crops of fruiting heads are yielded by a tree in full bearing each year, but the autumn crop is heavier than the earlier one, and the aggregate weight of fruit yielded by a tree in one year is generally estimated at 40 lbs.

The fruiting heads consist of large bunches which hang from near the crown of the tree, and each fruit is partly enveloped in a husk-like covering. When removed from this it is found to be smooth, somewhat conical or irregularly compressed, tapering towards an abrupt point. The colour when fresh varies from orange-red to nearly white, with a more or less broad black apex. In section it appears to be composed of a thick fibrous layer over a hard, somewhat rounded stone, which contains a whitish kernel. It is from the fibrous portion, which is included in what is botanically termed the pericarp, that the oil is obtained, but the kernel also contains another valuable oil, for the extraction of which it is shipped to Europe to a large extent.

Preparation of Palm Oil.—When the ripe head has been cut from the tree, it is left upon the ground for a few days in order that a shrinkage in the fruits may occur, which renders them more easily dislodged from their husk-lined places. The fruit also becomes slightly dull in colour. The heads bearing the fruit are often beaten to remove the latter, or they are individually broken out by hand. In order to facilitate the extraction of the fruit kernels, the fruits are usually buried in the ground in a pit lined with plantain leaves. Here they remain for from three weeks to a month, during which time decomposition is set up. The subsequent quality of the oil is dependent upon the degree to which this is allowed to proceed, rancid and thick oils resulting when it has been overdone. On the other hand, the higher the state of decomposition the greater is the facility for separating the fibrous pulp from the stones. On removing the fruits from the ground they are placed in an open vat (Fig. 15) and pounded by a number of people using long poles, after which they are covered up for several hours in order that the oil may drain into the small well shown at the side. Several consecutive poundings are applied, until the fibrous pulp is quite separated and most of the oil has drained out, after which the stones are combed out with the fingers, and the pulp is placed in a bag and pressed on a horizontal bar until the oil flows from it into a pit below. The oils from these extractions are boiled and cleared, and the residual pulp is often placed in the boiling pot so as to extract as much oil as possible. This is the method employed at the Krobo Plantations, but the operation varies slightly in different districts.

Kernel Oil—The value of the kernel for the extraction of oil was recognised at a much later date than the pericarp, although, in a few places in the Gold Coast, oil had probably been expressed from kernels for local consumption for some time. Among the Krobos the medicine-men prevented the trade in kernels from becoming established for several years, but they were finally overruled by the chiefs. A large and increasing trade in kernels continued for a number of years, but this has fallen off to a small extent more recently. The shell of the variety of kernel which appears to be the most common in this country is usually thick, and the laborious work of cracking each stone individually between two stones, in such a manner that the kernel is extracted in an unbroken state, prevents a larger quantity being prepared for sale, and results in much waste. Nut-cracking machines have been brought into the country, and are said to prove successful to some extent, but the native is not in a position to use machinery, and most of the material shipped is extracted in the primitive method mentioned. Cf. *Bulletin of the Imperial Institute*, vols. vii., viii. and xv. (1909-17). Before the cracking can be accomplished without breaking the interior, the kernel requires to be exposed to the sun and thoroughly dried. Kernel oil prepared in a native way is of two kinds, one which expressed without heat being white, whilst that made from the roasted kernels is dark brown. Both are made by pounding and grinding the kernel into fine meal, the extraction of the one being effected by cold and the other by boiling water.

In 1916 a Special Committee was appointed to consider the position of the palm-kernel trade, chiefly with reference to the protection of the newly-established British oil-crushing industry against German competition; and it was considered advisable to recommend the imposition of a differential export duty of £2 per ton on all palm kernels from British West African ports. The Colonies concerned imposed the duty at the rate mentioned and in some instances have since supplemented it by a direct revenue-producing tax.

Commercial Uses.—The chief commercial uses of the oils are for the manufacture of soap, candles, and glycerine, some qualities of palm oil being made use of in the manufacture of tin plates. With improved methods the supply of palm oil and kernels could be largely increased.

Varieties of Oil Palms.—In 1907 information was obtained from the Imperial Institute that a variety of oil palm was being propagated in the Kameruns the fruit of which contained a thin-shelled kernel and was called "Lisombe." Further investigation in the British West African countries led to the discovery that a number of well-marked varieties of *Elæis guineensis* were distinguished by the natives, and were called by distinct names. Among these one possessed a thin-shelled kernel, and, together with about eight others, has been under investigation at the Imperial Institute, with the object of ascertaining their respective merits. The thin-shelled "Lisombe" and the "Gamopale" varieties from the Kameruns have recently been tried experimentally in the Gold Coast, and the advantages they possess over the other kinds have been clearly established. From the descriptions given below of the more important varieties found on the Gold Coast, it will be seen that particulars of the comparative weight of the fruit crop and the quality of the oil yielded are required to determine the relative values. In addition the proportions of fruit- and kernel-oil of each as well as the facilities for extracting the kernel must be considered.

A reference is given below to six varieties, which have been fully examined at the Imperial Institute. The native names are given, and the percentages have been calculated for comparison, from the more elaborate figures which have been published (*Bulletin Imperial Institute*, vol. vii. [1909], p. 366; cf. also vol. xi. [1913], p. 208).

The characteristic variations of each variety are as follows:—

1. "Abe-pa." Fruit large, orange-red, with or without black tip, pericarp thin, nut large with thick shell. This is the commonest form in the country, and is probably identical with the variety found in Sierra Leone.

2. "Abe-dam." Fruit of irregular shape, fairly large, bright red, pericarp slightly thicker than the last, nut large with a thick shell. This is not uncommon.

3. "Abe-tuntum." Fruit moderately large, dark purplish-black, pericarp very thin, and nut with thick shell. Uncommon.

4. "Abe-bobe." Fruit usually rather small, red and black, pericarp thick and soft, nut with a thin kernel (easily broken in

the teeth). Trees rather scarce. This is probably identical with the "Lisombe" variety from the Kameruns.

5. "Intermediate form between 2 and 4." Similar to the last but with a thicker shell to the nut.

6. "Seedless kind." A very rare kind, nearly corresponding with the "Difumbe" variety from Angola, which, however, possesses a kernel but no shell.

The following are the percentages based on the total weight of the fruit, in each case taken as 100:—

Name	Pulp	Contg. oil	Fibre etc.	Nut	Contg. Kernel	Shell
1. "Abe-pa"	30	20·13	9·87	70	19·6	50·4
2. "Abe-dam"	37·5	24·03	13·14	62·5	16·87	45·63
3. "Abe-tuntum"	32·5	14·33	18·17	67·5	17·55	49·95
4. "Abe-bobe"	63	36·02	26·98	37	19·98	17·02
5. "Interm. 2 and 4"	51	30·34	20·66	49	20·58	28·42
6. "Seedless"	100	76·00	24·00		rarely a trace	

Nos. 4 and 5 seem to be most valuable from a commercial standpoint, although at present Nos. 1 and 2 are the most commonly used, owing to the comparative scarcity of the first two mentioned. No. 6 is chiefly interesting from a botanical aspect, and is probably incapable of reproduction. The sacred palm known in the Gold Coast as "Abe-ohene," and identical with "Ope-Ifa" of Southern Nigeria, belongs to a new species called *E. Thompsonii*, Chev., but the fruits are not employed for the extraction of oil.

OTHER OIL SEEDS.—Experiments were conducted at the Imperial Institute in 1908 with the kernels of the "Crabnut" (*Carapa procera*, D.C.). The kernels were found to contain nearly

50 per cent. of oil, which was reported to be worth about £20 10*s*. per ton, but the residual cake could not be used for feeding purposes, owing to the presence in it of a bitter constituent, and, on account of the rather low manurial value, was estimated as worth only £2 per ton (*Bulletin of the Imperial Institute*, vol. vi., 1908, p. 362).

The oil seemed to be well suited for soap-making, but would not be suitable for lubricating or for edible purposes. The nut does not occur in such profusion as to warrant profitable exportation from localities where the oil palm is found.

TIMBER. Mahogany.—The most valuable and commonly exported timber is that known in the European and American markets as "African Mahogany." The value of that shipped from the Gold Coast in 1913 was estimated at £366,000.

Several red woods are included under the name of Mahogany, but the best quality is said to be obtained from *Khaya senegalensis*, a large tree of the Natural Order *Meliaceæ*. This tree is known by the native (Fanti) name of "Dubini." In the same language the names "Okumankra" and "Akwabohori" are applied to two trees which are said to be exported as Mahogany, but of these the identity has not yet been determined.

Other Timber-trees.—The "Odum" tree (*Chlorophora excelsa*) produces a hard and useful wood, which is much used in the forest region, but is not often shipped (Fig. 19). In the dry country of the Northern Territories *Pseudocedrela Kotschyi* may be found of value as a red wood for decorative purposes.

Among the other trees which show evidence of yielding hard and useful woods are "Ahedua" (*Cyanothyrsus sp.*), "Opapeh" (*Afzelia africana*), and "Bako" (*Mimusops sp.*). Information about the working-quality and suitability for export of these and other Gold Coast timbers is given in the *Bulletin of the Imperial Institute*, vol. viii., 1910. p. 232.

The largest, and consequently the most valuable, trees belonging to the different species mentioned, are found in the western part of the Gold Coast and Ashanti, and most of the mahogany logs are shipped from Sekondi, Axim, and other places farther to the westward. The Pra and Ankobra rivers are utilised to float down the squared logs, which are then moored at the river mouths, to await shipment. The export of logs is only limited by the facilities with which they can be brought to a river or the railway, and large, valuable trees are plentiful in many of the forests, although they would be unprofitable to fell and trim in some cases, owing to their remote situations and the difficulties connected with conveyance.

KOLA.—Kola-nut is the name usually applied to the fruit of a tree belonging to the Natural Order *Sterculiaceæ*, and the wild as well as the cultivated forms found in the Gold Coast and Ashanti are, probably, all referable to the species *Kola acuminata*, R. The fruits or nuts are borne in large pods, each of which contains a variable number. The nuts themselves are irregular in form, and have an inconstant number of cotyledons, or seed divisions, varying from two to five. Some confusion seems to have been caused owing to this variation, as well as on account of the colour and shape of the nuts. In some trees they are red, in others white, and others again pink, and they may be elongate or nearly round. These, however, are not reliable as distinguishing characters, since nuts of the three colours have been found on the same tree, and even in the same pod. Analyses and commercial valuations of several varieties of kola nuts from the Gold Coast are published in *Selected Reports from* the *Imperial Institute*, Part III., "Foodstuffs" (Colonial Reports, Misc., Cd. 5137, 1910), pp. 259-61; *vide* also *Bull. Imp. Inst.*, vols. x. (1912) and xvii. (1919).

In the forests to the north of Kumassi large wild kola trees are found, and the nuts are collected by the natives inhabiting the villages in the vicinity, where they are sold at from 6*d*. to 9*d*. a hundred. In other places the trees are planted, commonly on the outskirts of villages, especially in Akim and Kwahu.

Kola nuts are used in tropical Africa in the same manner as betel nuts are in Asia. Their taste is somewhat bitter, and the mastication of fresh nuts seems to increase the flow of saliva. Chewing kola nuts is resorted to by the natives in order to allay thirst, or even hunger, and for this reason they are in great demand among the inhabitants of the Sudan, to which country they are largely exported, being carried by men and donkeys in caravans, which travel from the forest limits of Ashanti through the Northern Territories. The donkeys, which are chiefly used to transport the nuts, do not generally enter the forests, but the kola nuts are packed in elongated head-loads, in bamboo or palm-stalk frames, in which form they are carried to the place where the donkeys have been left. The caravans bring shea-butter, guinea corn, cattle, and skins, which they exchange for kola.

The weight of nuts exported from the Gold Coast is about 50 per cent. above that of Sierra Leone, but, in value, the latter are worth from three to five times as much per ton. The fresh nuts are shipped to Lagos and are transported far into the interior by Haussa traders.

COTTON.—No record is available to show when the tribes of the forest country commenced to cultivate and use cotton for local requirements. It has been stated that the people of the kingdoms of the Western Sudan were acquainted with the uses of the fibre, and have cultivated the plant, from a remote period, and it is probable that contact with these people, during their expeditions against the tribes to their south, led to the adoption by the latter of cotton-growing upon the small scale in which it still remains at present. Cruickshank, writing of the Fantis in 1853, says: "They spin the thread from the cotton which grows in the country, but they more commonly make use of the thread out of English cloths, which they pick to pieces." In speaking of the Appolonians, a tribe inhabiting the coast region near Axim, Cruickshank remarks that they "make fine grass cloths, which are strong and durable." In Ashanti, until recently, a cloth was commonly made from the inner bark of a tree, generally supposed to be *Antiaris toxicaria* var. *africana*, which was produced by the removal of the woody portions by beating, leaving a pliable material composed of the interlacing fibres. These instances are cited to show that the value of cotton for cultivation has not been recognised by some of the large and dominant tribes in comparatively recent times. Since cotton clothing has begun to be appreciated, the necessity of growing the plant and weaving has been somewhat checked by the large imports of finished material from Europe.

Throughout the forest region occasional plants of cotton may be seen growing near villages, but the systematic cultivation of the plant is only met with on the outer northern boundary of the dense forest and in the Krepi country to the east of the Volta river. The inhabitants of the northern forest boundary are a mixed people, many of whom have probably been driven from the countries farther north, where cotton is a recognised field crop, whence they have introduced the cultivation. The adoption of cotton-growing by the Krepi tribes may be due to similar reasons, although there appears to be no evidence in support of this conjecture.

In the last-named places the seed is sown in rows on the tops of ridges, on the sides of which maize plants may be also grown, but it is not uncommon to find cotton plants growing alone. This is especially the case on the northern limits of Ashanti. The large varieties grown in these places are often left in the ground for a second season and produce two crops, the last of which is said to be inferior. No system of rotation has been observed, although it is probable that the cotton is planted during the early years of cultivation immediately following the yam crop, which is the practice in some other West African countries.

Three distinct forms or varieties of cotton are cultivated in the forest region. The first variety is usually referred to as "Green seed," and is the commonest one grown. The lint is long-stapled and nearly white, but experiments seem to show that this form does not yield heavily. The second form is recognised by the seed being dark brown or black, without any fuzz, except a small brown tuft at the apex, which has a sharp spike. The lint of this kind is creamy white, and the plant is known as "Volta." The third form differs in having the dark brown seeds adjoining one another, and forming a conical mass, from which it is difficult to separate the individual seeds. At the point of connection each seed bears a small light brown patch. This form is generally known to the officers at the British Cotton Growing Association plantation as "Kidney." All these varieties are cultivated throughout the forest country, and extend to some distance beyond; being replaced in the drier parts of the Northern Territories by a small plant with a white woolly seed. No cotton in a wild state has been seen in the country, and isolated plants, found springing up in open places surrounded by forest, are generally easily traceable to formerly existing cultivation.

The "Green seed," "Volta," and "Kidney" cottons, which are grown in the Gold Coast, are different in habit from the American and Indian plants, although in form they are similar to Sea Island and Egyptian, having, perhaps, arisen from the same original stock. The forms mentioned as cultivated locally attain the height of from seven to ten feet in nine months from the time of planting, and the stem near the base is often thicker than a man's wrist. The cotton bolls continue to open for three months or more, and often as many as two hundred bolls are produced on a single plant in one season. If left for a second year the bolls are generally diminished in size. The soil which appears most favourable for growth is a sandy loam containing much humus.

From January to April the bolls ripen continuously, and the cotton is placed in the sun as soon as it is picked, in order that the "Seed bugs" may be driven out. In native markets small quantities are usually exposed for sale in an unginned form throughout the harvesting season. No gin seems to be in use in the Gold Coast for native work, and the lint is pulled off the seeds by hand when a supply is required for spinning.

The greatest damage is done by "Seed bugs" of three species—*Oxycarenus hyalinipennis, O. Dudgeoni*, and *O. gossipinus*—that infest the lint as soon as the bolls open, and undergo their complete and rapid metamorphoses during the period between the opening and the throwing out of the cotton, feeding meanwhile upon the juices which they suck from the seeds. The injury caused by the puncturing of the seed often renders it unfertile. A "cotton stainer" is also common on the plants, and damages the unopened bolls by puncturing, and the lint by a yellowish stain which it makes. This insect is known as *Dysdercus nigrofasciatus*, and it is at least four times as large as any of the species of *Oxycarenus*, on which it may possibly feed to some extent.

An attempt was evidently made, in the middle of the last century, to establish the cultivation of cotton for export, and Cruickshank mentions that an association had taken the matter up, and that several of the native chiefs were beginning to give it their attention about that time. Very little success seems to have attended these efforts.

About 1903 the Government of the Gold Coast commenced the plantation of an area in the Krepi country, at a place called Anum, and, under the control of the Agricultural Department, this was transferred to a better site soon afterwards, at a place named Labolabo on the east bank of the Volta river. In addition to the extension of about two hundred acres of land, which were planted with native and American varieties of cotton, encouragement was given to the natives in the vicinity to grow more, on the understanding that their crops would be purchased from them at one penny per pound. Unfortunately no arrangements had been made to store or gin a large quantity of seed cotton, and the entire native crop could not be taken over when brought in. This seems to have induced the native growers to convey most of their cotton into Togoland, where they were able to dispose of it at a fair price. Arrangements had to be made with a local firm possessing a ginning machine, which was erected about sixty miles lower down the Volta river, by which, on payment of a certain rate, the seed cotton grown on the Labolabo plantation was ginned and prepared for shipment. It was soon recognised that the expense of transport of the seed cotton for this distance, and the price charged for ginning, prevented the production of cotton for export except at a heavy financial loss. The co-operation of the British Cotton Growing Association was asked for, in order to supply gins at Labolabo, and in 1906 three hand gins were sent from the Gold Coast Exhibition, which had just been held. The machines were much damaged in transit, and it was some time before the large stock of seed cotton, which had accumulated, could be worked off. Soon after this the Labolabo plantation was transferred entirely to the British Cotton Growing Association, and an annual grant was made by the Government to assist in the working. In 1907 a large steam-power ginnery was put up, and the native farmers again began to bring in their seed cotton for sale, but still a considerable quantity was reported to be diverted to Togoland, where the price offered was a fraction higher than that paid by the Association.

The cotton bales are transported from the ginnery by means of native canoes as far as Amedika, which is the highest point on the Volta to which small steamers can ascend, but great risk is entailed in descending the rapids between Labolabo and this place. The cost of carriage by native canoe is arranged at twenty shillings a ton, and the bales are pressed into a suitable form for conveyance.

American and other Exotic Cottons at Labolabo.—A large number of different kinds of American cottons have been tried at Labolabo, but most of them have proved unsuccessful. Those which yielded a good crop for the first year have generally been found to produce seed, which, owing to the greater susceptibility of the plants to the attacks of insects, refused to germinate in the following year. Some of the lint produced was, apparently, of excellent quality and sold well, but the necessity for the renewal of seed each year formed a serious obstacle to the establishment of a new variety. The plants from American seed are not so hardy as those from native seed, and the necessity for greater care in cultivation renders them unsuitable for use by the natives. Sea Island and various Egyptian cottons have not proved successful. See *British Cotton Cultivation*, by Professor Dunstan ("Colonial Reports," Miscellaneous, Cd. 3997, 1908, pp. 28-30), and the *Bulletins of the Imperial Institute*, vols. vii., x., xi., xiii., xiv. (1909-16).

Attempts at Hybridisation.—In the early days of the plantation the Agricultural Department made several experiments with a view to the establishment of a cross between the native and the American plants, but the subsequent changes in the management of the plantation resulted in the disappearance of most of these; subsequently several others were attempted in 1906 and 1907 by Mr. Fisher.

In all cases plants of the "Green seed" or the "Volta" native forms were made use of as female parents, and the descendant plants partook of the characters of the native forms in every way for the first generation, but in later generations seem to have produced a number of various types, from which it is now necessary to make a careful selection. The quantity of lint yielded by the first generation of plants, from the experiments made by Mr. Fisher in 1906, is said to have reached a higher figure, per acre, than that of any other form grown on the plantation, and the quality was satisfactory; but that of the second generation appeared to be unequal in type, and could scarcely be compared for quantity owing to the unfavourable season. The American plants used for pollination in the 1906 crosses were those which have given the best results among the exotic forms planted, and are called "Black Rattler" and "Richmond." Of the four crosses attempted in that year, that of "Black Rattler" × "Volta" was said to have proved the most successful in point of yield.

Small plots of native and American cottons have been planted at Kumassi, and experimental plants at Aburi, but the conditions have not been so favourable at these places as at Labolabo. At Obuassi, in Ashanti, an attempt was also made, but the soil seemed too stiff and the plants were not healthy. Land suitable for native cotton farms seems to be that on the west bank of the Volta river, north of the Labolabo plantation.

Valuations of Samples examined at the Imperial Institute.—The following selection of specimens of Gold Coast cottons examined and reported on at different times by the Imperial Institute will give some indication of the relative values:—

Place	Variety	Staple	Value	Standard at time of valuation "Middl. Amer."
Labolabo	Volta clean-seed	0·8-1·4	5-5½d.	5·05d.
,,	Green-seed	1-1·4	5d.	5·05d.
,,	Black Volta, small woolly seeded from N. Terr.	1-1·4	5½-6d.	6·43d.
,,	Black Rattler	1·2-1·8	7d.	6·7d.
,,	Native × Allens	1·2-1·6	6d.	,,
,,	Native × Russels	1·2-1·5	4½d.	,,
,,	Native × Peruvian	1·2-1·6	7d.	,,
,,	Native × Culpepper	1·1-1·5	6½-7d.	,,
,,	Volta × Black Rattler	1·1-1·5	5d.	,,
,,	Volta × Richmond	1·1-1·6	6-6½d.	,,
,,	Greenseed × Black Rattler	1-1·4	5d.	,,
,,	Greenseed × Richmond	1-1·4	7d.	,,
	Tamale, N. Terr., Native	0·7-1·0	5½d.	,,

The cottons from native varieties crossed with American represent the first generation only, as in no case were the following generations found constant.

The large profits which have been made from cocoa in the forest country have caused cotton-growing to be neglected, and it seems improbable that large quantities of cotton will be exported from this region during the next few years. In the same part of the country palm oil and rubber are easily collected, and, besides being more remunerative products, require comparatively small exertion in preparation. An attempt to establish cotton cultivation upon a commercial scale, among the industrious people of the Northern Territories, was made by the British Cotton Growing Association, but the immense distances of the inhabited tracts from a shipping port and the consequent expense of transport, combined with the uncertainty of the rainfall in these ultra-forest regions, compelled the abandonment of the venture in 1916.

FIBRES.—Piassava fibre, which has sometimes been called "vegetable whalebone," is prepared from the sheath of the lower parts of the leaf-stem of a tree belonging to the Natural Order *Palmæ*, and classified as *Raphia vinifera*, P. Beauv. This tree is found growing in the vicinity of streams, and occurs commonly in the forest regions near the coast.

The natives prepare the fibre, which is sold in the European markets under the name of "Piassava," by cutting the stem-sheaths and steeping them in water for a considerable time until the fibrous strands are easily separated by beating. After being extracted in this manner they are dried in the sun. Only a small quantity is exported from the country, but it is a more important article of export from Sierra Leone and Liberia. As the specific name denotes, wine is extracted from the tree, by tapping the standing or felled tree, in the last case with the aid of fire.

On the estate of the African Plantations, Ltd., near Axim, a fibre of excellent quality, commercially allied to jute, has been prepared from the stems of a herbaceous plant, which was supposed to be *Triumfetta semitriloba*, Linn., but which has since been determined at Kew to be *T. cordifolia* var. *Hollandii*, Sprague. The plant belongs to the same Natural Order as Indian jute—namely, *Tiliaceæ*. A description of this fibre is given in the *Bulletin of the Imperial Institute*, vol. vi. (1908), p. 241.

This species has been observed commonly in a wild state in the forests near Sekondi and Axim, but does not seem to be present in the interior of Ashanti or in the country towards the Volta river.

Experiments made at the estate of the African Plantations, Ltd., are said to show that the best fibre is obtained from stalks which have been retted or steeped in water for five days, but it will probably be found that the period required for the operation is dependent to a great extent upon the age of the stalks used.

The fibre may be prepared by stripping the bark layers from the soaked stalks and beating these upon the surface of the water until the actual bark is removed, when the fibre may be dried in the sun; being finally picked over to get rid of the small remaining bark particles.

The plant exhibits some advantages for cultivation over jute, in that it may be cropped twice in one year and treated as a perennial. Collection of the wild growths would be unsatisfactory for the production of the fibre upon a large scale, owing to the time occupied in searching for the plants, but it seems probable that the plant would repay planting, especially if some better method of extraction were devised.

The composition, quality, and commercial value of a large number of fibres obtained from plants indigenous to, or cultivated in, the Gold Coast are discussed in *Selected Reports from the Imperial Institute*, Part I., "Fibres" (Colonial Reports, Miscellaneous, Cd. 4588, 1909), pp. 43, 51, 84, 89, 90, 115.

SILK.—A species of wild silkworm is commonly distributed throughout the forests to the north of Kumassi, and has been identified as *Anaphe venata*. The silk cocoons of this species and those of *Anaphe infracta* are used in Nigeria for spinning into yarn for weaving the "Sanyan" cloths of that country, but no use is apparently made of them in Ashanti. The worms live in small colonies, and form their cocoons in a common envelope of silk, from which two or three somewhat tubular processes project to enable the moths to emerge when the time arrives. The food plant of the silkworm has not been definitely ascertained, but, as the cocoons are found on a large number of herbaceous plants as well as trees, it seems probable that several plants are eaten by it. The quality of the silk is said to be good, and the colour is usually a golden or light brown.[3]

COPAL.—The tree which produces this resin, often miscalled "gum," which is commercially known as "Accra copal," occurs throughout the forests of Ashanti and Akim, and has not yet been specifically determined. Investigations have shown that it is allied to *Cyanothyrsus oblongus*, Oliver, which yields the "Ogea" resin of Lagos, and which belongs to the Natural Order *Leguminosæ*. The flowers obtained from the Ashanti trees are of a similar construction to those of *Cyanothyrsus*.

Locally the resin is commonly used for torches and for

the preparation of a scented pigment called "Krobo," which is used for elaborating patterns upon the skin, being commonly employed by the Akim people for this purpose. For export the chief value is for the preparation of varnish.

The quantity exported reached 178 tons in 1907, after which it declined, and now no longer reaches a significant figure. The overwhelming interest attracted by cocoa has led to its disappearance. Cf. *Selected Reports Imperial Institute*, pt. ii., "Gums and Resins" (Col. Rep. Misc., Cd. 4971, 1909), pp. 172-5; *Bull. Imp. Inst.*, vol. xii. (1914), p. 220.

The copal-yielding trees are generally of immense size, and the resinous liquid may be observed exuding from the main trunk as well as the branches, in such a way as to form elongated "tears" or slabs, which harden on exposure to the air. When these become brittle they are broken off by wind and fall to the ground. Often the flow of resinous liquid seems to be so profuse that quantities reach the ground and form what is termed "fossil copal," owing to the fact that it is dug from the ground beneath the trees.

There is evidence to show that in some instances the original flow of the resinous liquid is caused by deep borings in the sap wood made by insect larvæ (probably *Coleoptera*—beetles), signs of which are commonly apparent on old trees, which yield the most copal. Specimens of branches, which have been tunnelled by these larvæ, have been collected, exhibiting all the cavities filled with hardened resin.

Compared with the copal produced by *Copaifera Guibourtiana*, a tree which is found in Sierra Leone, the Ashanti product is much inferior, although the price paid renders it sufficiently valuable for collection and export. Several different types of the Accra copal are known, some of which appear to be of less value than others, although apparently yielded by the same tree. That which is deemed preferable is clear and pale yellow; milky pieces should be sorted out, as they are valued at a lower figure. Blocks have been obtained which weighed over twenty pounds. Sorting is said to have been adopted by some of the local merchants, and as high a price as 60*s*. per cwt. is reported to have been obtained for sorted copal.

COPRA.—Some special attention has been given to the extension of the copra industry on the coast, and it will be observed that the average annual exports have nearly doubled during the last eight years. The coconut (*Cocos nucifera*) is found on the greater part of the coastline, and the dried contents of the nut constitute the product known as copra. (Cf. *Oil Seeds and Feeding Cakes*, Imp. Inst. Monograph, 1915.) No use is apparently made of the fibrous covering of the nuts, which is exported from other parts of the world under the name of coir. Locally the nuts are cut down in an unripe condition, and the "milk" from the interior is used as a drink.

DYES AND PIGMENTS.—Camwood is the trade name applied to the wood of a tree known as *Baphia nitida*, Afzelius, belonging to the Natural Order *Leguminosæ*. It has been suggested that the bright red colouring-matter is produced by decomposition on exposure to air, the material shipped from different places in West Africa being apparently in this condition, but investigations in other parts of West Africa show that the fresh wood is frequently used in making the colouring-matter. A very small quantity is exported from the Gold Coast, but the natives make some use of it for staining different materials.

Indigo.—This is prepared from two or three species of

Indigofera, which are found growing near villages, but the process of preparation in the Gold Coast does not appear to have been recorded, though probably similar to that employed in the other West African countries.

The resin from the copal tree, mentioned above, is crushed, together with the bark of a tree called "Krobo," in Akim especially, and the balls formed from this mixture are rubbed down, with the addition of a little water, into a fine sort of lather, when a greenish-grey-coloured thin paste is procured. With this designs are traced upon the body and arms as an adornment for women, the resin imparting to the mixture a pleasant odour.

FIELD CROPS.—The soil throughout a large part of the forest country is very fertile, and no difficulty is experienced in producing sufficient crops for local needs from a small area of ground. The usual method is to cut down a piece of forest, leaving those trees which are too large to be removed or burnt, or which may yield one of the wild fruits which is appreciated. The stumps and roots are not removed when only maize (*Zea mays*) is intended to be grown, but are, to some extent, when yams (*Dioscorea sp.*), or groundnuts (*Arachis hypogea*), are to be cultivated. The cut "bush" is permitted to dry in the sun for several weeks, when it is burned, and the ashes are sometimes scattered over the land. For plantations of maize, the soil is only turned up at the spots where the seed is to be put in, and very little cultivation is given for the remainder of the year, although weeding and earthing up are resorted to in a few places. For the cultivation of yams or groundnuts, the larger roots are dug out, and the whole field is dug with small hoes, the soil being scraped together into small mounds, on the top of which the yams or groundnuts are planted. In the case of the former, stakes are also put in, upon which the yams are trained to grow. In addition to this it is usual, in most places, to plant maize upon the sides of the mounds, and okra (*Hibiscus esculentus*) and peppers (*Capsicum sp.*) in various parts of the field. Guinea corn (*Sorghum vulgare*) is rarely seen within the forest limits. Between the mounds, at wide intervals, plantains (*Musa sapientum*) are generally grown, and occupy the ground after all the other crops have been removed. In the country near the coast, as well as in the Volta district, cassava (*Manihot utilissima*) is a common terminal crop, although it is not frequently grown in Ashanti. The length of time during which the land usually continues to yield a grain or root crop, of the kinds above mentioned, seems limited to about three years. Koko yams (*Colocasia antiquorum*) are planted in damp places near the villages or beside streams, and, in the Volta district, sweet potatoes (*Ipomœa batatas*) are cultivated to a small extent. Small gourds (*Cucurbitaceæ*) are cultivated in the villages, but are not common, and pineapples, paw-paws, guavas, oranges, custard apples, sour-sops, and limes may be found growing in the places near the older European settlements.

Plantains and yams seem to form the chief food of the people in the interior, but maize is largely used by those near the coast, who are better cultivators. Plantains are prepared by roasting or by chopping up and boiling. In some parts, especially in the Krepi country, the fruits are split and cut in pieces, after which they are dried in the sun. They become hard and white in the process, and can be kept for some time. Yams of several kinds are cut up after peeling, and boiled with peppers or made up with palm oil, when they form a favourite dish. They are sometimes pounded in a wooden mortar and made into balls. Maize is ground on flat or grooved stones by means of a stone hand-roller, after which the flour is made into dough and baked, a little palm wine having been added to make it rise. Cassava is treated in the same manner as yams, but the former requires long soaking before cooking. Palm oil or groundnut oil is generally used for cooking, and the pulp of the palm fruit, after the oil has been removed, is eaten. A fermented drink is made from maize, which is said to taste like weak beer, but the chief intoxicant made locally is the fermented juice of the oil and the fibre palms.

With the exception of cotton, which has been separately referred to, groundnuts appear to have been the only field crop of importance that has been exported. In 1908 a substantial figure was reached, but has since declined.

PART II.—THE NORTHERN TERRITORIES

Tribes.—The country which is included under the Northern Territories is inhabited by a number of tribes, now chiefly located in the northern half; the central portion being liable to inundation at certain times, and therefore almost unoccupied, and the southern being, perhaps, considered unsafe owing to the proximity to the warlike Ashantis. The more important tribes are the Mamprussis, under the king of Gambaga; the Gonjas, under the king of Kombe; the Walas, under the king of Wa; and two sections of the Dagombas, under the chiefs of Savelugu and Karaga (formerly under the king of Yendi, in German territory). The Lobis, Dagartis, Grunshis, Kussassis, and several others were dispersed by Samory and Barbetu in 1896 and 1898, and have now only nominal chiefs. (See *Colonial Reports—Annual*, No. 566, "Northern Territories of the Gold Coast," 1907, p. 8.) The Moshis, whose country extended into the northern limits of the Northern Territories, were employed at one time as native levies, but since they were disbanded they have interfered with the tribes on the Gambaga-Kumassi road, in the Sapari Hills, and made trading by that route unsafe. (See *Colonial Reports, loc. cit.*, p. 10.) Steps have been taken to expel them from the country, and it is hoped that the people living in the hills, who are said to be good agriculturists, will now come into closer contact with civilisation. The Dagombas are apparently the most industrious tribe in the country, and they seem to be numerous.

Although there does not appear to be any actual record of the invasion of the eastern part of the country by the Mohammedan rulers of the Western Sudan, they are said to have overrun the pagan countries between themselves and the region of dense forest on several occasions. In 1483 the kingdom of Mossi (Moshi) was conquered by Sonni Ali, King of Songhay, who was a native of the Eastern Sudan, and had come from Egypt. Two years later he extended his conquest through the mountain territory to the south and far into the pagan belt. Sonni Ali was followed by Askia, who again overran Mossi, in order to abolish paganism and establish the Mohammedan faith. This occurred in about the year 1500, and doubtless the people learnt to adopt the improved methods of agriculture which the conquerors had introduced into the Western Sudan from Egypt and the east. Many of the tribes have relapsed completely into paganism, but amongst others there is a mixture of Mohammedanism and paganism, which is evidence of the impression made. More recently, Samodu Almami of Ouassoulou, generally known as Samory, was driven from his kingdom in the Western Sudan by the French, and overran the Northern Territories with his Sofa troops; subduing Wa, Bole, and the whole of the western part of the country. It is, however, unlikely that agriculture was further improved by his invasion, as large tracts of country were devastated to feed his troops.

FIELD CROPS.—The soil is of a lighter and more sandy nature than that generally found in the forest region, but it is well adapted for the cultivation of many different kinds of crops, notably Guinea corn, millet, groundnuts, and cotton, while it is less satisfactory for yams. The latter are consequently of smaller size.

Cotton.—The cotton grown by the Dagombas is whiter than those found in the south, and the plants are of small stature; the species has a wide-opening pale flower, and has been grown at Labolabo from seed procured in the Northern Territories. The cotton fields are planted with regular lines of plants, and the ground appears to be exclusively used for the crop during the season. The seed is sown upon ridges which have been constructed from the high conical mounds, upon which the combined crop of millet (*Pennisetum spp.*) or Guinea corn and yams were grown in the previous year. Cultivation is performed by means of a short-handled hoe, and the ridges are kept clear of weeds and grass until the crop is ready. The seed-cotton is sold in the markets, and is in good demand for the manufacture of native cloths. No insect pests have been observed attacking the plants, and it is probable that if an outside demand were established for the produce a large quantity could be grown. It might be necessary to introduce a better variety than that at present cultivated, as this yields a rather coarse and short staple. If cotton from this part of the country is to become an article of export, the difficulties at present experienced in transport will first have to be overcome; indeed, this applies to all the produce capable of being grown in the country. The navigation of the Volta river and the two main branches seems to suggest a means which might be employed, for, although there are several rapids in the course from Daboya and Bole to Labolabo, only one is impassable for canoes, even in the dry season. This rapid is at Krachi where a short line has been laid for transporting loaded canoes. The cost of the hire of canoes for making the journey would probably be prohibitive, but if the British Cotton Growing Association undertook the carriage by their own canoes of the salt and stores required by the merchants who have commenced business in Yeji and Tamale, the freight on these in the journey upwards would probably be found to cover the cost of bringing cotton down-stream, and the export trade in it could be developed in this manner. The British Cotton Growing Association made an effort to act upon the suggestion made here, but discontinued their operations in July 1916, when they handed over their buildings, at Tamale, to the Government, as it was shown that under the existing conditions and with but one European representative to further its interests, cotton-growing in the Northern Territories could not hope to become a remunerative export business (Colonial Reports, Northern Territories, G.C. 1916, No. 956). The irregularity of the rainfall is a matter which must be borne in mind in any future attempts to develop the industry here, but the possibilities of providing artificial irrigation should not be overlooked, as large tracts of flat land exist near the White Volta river capable of becoming fertile under proper irrigation and drainage.

Other Field Crops.—Yams are grown as a primary crop on mounds, and three different kinds are common, probably referable to *D. alata*, *D. sativa*, and *D. colocasiæfolia*, the last being what is termed the water yam and the first the winged yam. Guinea corn is the most important food grain grown, but millet is sometimes planted. A red species of sorghum (*S. guineensis*, var. *robustum*) is cultivated on a small scale for use in staining leather, but is not used for food. Rice (*Oryza sativa*) is grown in the vicinity of the large rivers, but is said to suffer damage from elephants and hippopotami. The variety seems to be similar to the red rice grown in the Gambia and Sierra Leone. Very little maize is planted, but some is grown near Salaga. Cassava is only seen in the south near the forest boundary, and groundnuts are not plentiful, owing, perhaps, to the fact that cooking oil is obtainable from shea butter trees, which are common in a wild state. Pigeon peas are often planted round the borders of fields, and are left to yield more than one crop. This pea is identical with one of the common "Dhalls" of India (*Cajanus indicus*); the origin of the introduction is obscure. Small beans are grown as well as *Indigofera spp.* Sweet potatoes, okra, capsicum-peppers, sorrel-hibiscus (*H. Sabdariffa*), and the Fra-Fra potato (*Plectranthus, sp.*, "Tumuku" of the Haussas) are also grown.

Fibre.—Plants belonging to two species of *Hibiscus* are used for the extraction of fibre for the preparation of cordage, the cleaned fibre being similar to jute. These plants grow, with perfectly straight stems, to eight or ten feet in height, bearing short thin branches with axillary flowers.

Tobacco.—The tobacco grown is used for smoking or the manufacture of snuff in many parts of the Northern Territories, and is prepared in a special manner. For smoking tobacco the green leaves are pressed into small gourds until a quantity of juice exudes, the mass being rolled in this until it assumes an oval form, in which it is sold in the markets before drying. For snuff it is ground up between heated stones until the requisite fineness has been obtained, and is then mixed with a small quantity of the powdered seeds of *Monodora myristica*. The tobacco fields are usually confined to small patches near houses, and wood ashes as well as sweepings are applied as a top dressing. This appears to be the only crop to which manure or fertiliser is given. The leaves always seem to be stripped off the stems at one operation, whereby old and immature leaves are mixed with mature.

GUMS.—Two species of *Acacia* (*A. arabica* and *A. Sieberiana*) are found, especially in the uninhabited tracts in the centre of the country, and the last named appears to yield a large flow of gum, which, however, is not collected. Examination of this at the Imperial Institute has shown it to be about equal in quality to inferior Sudan grades; *A. arabica* does not seem to yield gum with such frequency in this locality as elsewhere. *Burkea africana* and *Pseudocedrela Kotschyi* produce a quality of gum comparable with "Talh" from the Sudan. (Cf. *Selected Reports from the Imperial Institute*, Pt. II., Gums and Resins, pp. 153, 165-7.)

WOOD OIL.—By cutting deeply into the base of a tree known as "Neou" (Dagomba), and "Kawa" (Haussa), a rather copious flow of resinous liquid is induced, which, when solidified, is a resin somewhat similar, but inferior, to copal. The tree from which this is procured is botanically known as *Daniellia thurifera*, Oliv., and the so-called "oil" obtained was at one time shipped from Northern Nigeria under the name of African Balsam of Copaiba. It is used in the Northern Territories for lighting purposes, as well as medicinally. The tree yields a handsomely grained timber. (Cf. *Bull. Imp. Inst.*, 1915.)

SHEA BUTTER.—A tree known botanically as *Butyrospermum Parkii* bears a fruit, from the kernel of which this valuable vegetable fat is procured. The fat forms the cooking oil of the ultra-forest country, taking the place of palm oil in this respect. The mode of preparation in the Northern Territories is, doubtless, similar to that employed in Northern Nigeria. The prepared butter is one of the products carried by the Haussa traders, who visit Ashanti for the purpose of purchasing kola, and is much appreciated in Kumassi, where it obtains a high price. A small quantity is carried down the Volta river by the canoes which bring salt from Adda to Yeji and Daboya. An analysis made at the Imperial Institute of Shea butter from the Northern Territories showed that the material is in no way inferior to the better-known "Shea butter" of Northern Nigeria. Cf. *Bulletin of the Imperial Institute*, vol. vi. (1908), p. 370.

RUBBER.—Recently some species of *Landolphia* were found growing in the district of Wa and elsewhere, and, upon examination, one of these proved to be *L. owariensis*, P. Beauv. This was at first thought to occur plentifully, and to assume the underground habits of *L. Thollonii*, one of the most important sources of root or rhizome rubber in the Congo. Specimens, which were found growing near the south bank of the Black Volta river, in grass land, exhibited a trailing form of growth owing to the absence of supporting trees, but, although the plants were probably dwarfed by the annual grass fires, no development of root growth was observed in excess of that ordinarily produced within the forests. The plant is now reported to occur rather rarely in the Northern Territories; another nearly allied, though useless, species having been mistaken for it.

DYES.—For dyeing the yarn made from the native cotton, indigo is made from a species of *Indigofera*, or from the young leaves of *Lonchocarpus cyanescens*, but the process of preparation employed in this country has not been carefully observed. It is, however, probably similar to that in common use in Sierra Leone, Northern Nigeria, and the Gambia.

BEESWAX.—Bees are attracted to hive in calabashes placed in trees, the honey and wax being taken from them and sold in the markets. The bee belongs to a small variety of *Apis mellifera*, known as var. *Adansonii*. A sample of beeswax obtained at Tamale was examined at the Imperial Institute, and proved to be of excellent quality and worth £6 15*s*. per cwt. (Dec. 1908).

LEATHER.—Tanning of sheep and goats' skins is done to a small extent, the same process as that described for the preparation of Kano leather in Northern Nigeria being followed. The *Acacia* pods used for the purpose are obtained from trees often found planted in the middle of towns.

CATTLE AND POULTRY.—A large breed of cattle with a dorsal hump exists in the Salaga district, and a straight-backed smaller kind throughout the country to the north. Although "tsetse" flies of three species are common on the stream banks, the cattle seem to be healthy for the most part, and often form part of a caravan travelling to the forest belt, where a good price is said to be obtained for them from the Ashantis. They are usually killed for food very soon after entering the forest, where they can no longer be kept free from the attacks of the three species of "tsetse" (*Glossina morsitans*, *G. palpalis*, and *G. pallidipes*), all of which seem to attack them. Horses are bred in some parts, but not to a large extent. Wire-haired sheep and goats are seen everywhere, and can be obtained in many places at a low price.

Fowls and Guinea-fowls are reared in several villages, and

are carried to the south for sale. Long open-work baskets are used, and the fowls are usually conveyed as head-loads. Guinea-fowls, purchasable for threepence each in some of the villages south of Daboya, are sold at four or five shillings each near the coast. No coops seem to be employed in the villages to confine the guinea-fowls, which habitually roost upon the house-tops and which may frequently be seen in the adjoining fields. They are scarcely distinguishable from the wild birds which occur usually in the same localities. There is, however, a marked tendency on the part of the domesticated examples to acquire white feathers upon the breast or wings to a greater or lesser extent.

It should be recorded that a considerable local trade is carried on in the country in the sale of a flour-like substance obtained from the interior of the pods of *Parkia filicoidea*. This is made up with the seeds of the plant into an edible paste, locally termed "Dawadawa."

EXPORTS.—Excluding cocoa, which is treated separately in its place, the following table shows the progress of the export trade between 1910 and 1919:—

Year.	Kola. Lbs.	£	Copra. Tons.	£	Copal. Lbs.	£
1910	5,156,500	77,716	755	13,032	53,847	647
1911	5,791,931	93,099	779	13,257	80,042	1,110
1912	7,133,165	134,231	620	11,841	67,133	1,077
1913	7,024,868	144,705	629	14,292	38,205	555
1914	7,862,414	142,190	656	11,825	18,549	265
1915	8,267,100	139,163	770	12,821	28,888	405

1916	6,760,898	130,566	633	14,384	12,549	132	
1917	11,985,645	239,134	735	19,916	2,306	24	
1918	13,254,538	262,144	99	2,772	1,693	35	
1919	16,319,972	350,249	984	30,091	13,748	174	

	Rubber.		Palm Oil.		Palm Kernels.	
	Lbs.	£	Galls.	£	Tons.	£
1910	3,223,265	358,876	2,044,868	161,388	14,182	185,058
1911	2,668,667	219,447	1,610,209	128,916	13,254	175,891
1912	1,990,699	168,729	1,444,432	112,885	14,628	205,365
1913	1,317,369	87,915	860,155	65,652	9,744	159,128
1914	654,133	21,631	495,763	37,646	5,633	88,671
1915	647,982	25,167	330,990	25,769	4,064	50,512
1916	2,215,973	78,865	450,360	38,299	5,857	85,899
1917	2,961,204	110,272	198,900	24,770	4,768	74,911
1918	1,391,097	57,006	670,867	83,689	8,933	152,922
1919	721,588	33,637	938,595	140,163	9,892	253,243

	Lumber.		Cotton.		Groundnuts.	
	Feet.	£	Lbs.	£	Tons.	£
					1907:	
1910	14,938,749	148,122	11,421	263	197	1,815
1911	13,973,396	138,821	9,701	238	not given	
1912	23,573,651	228,745	20,395	506	do.	
1913	37,391,848	366,094	27,497	688	do.	

1914	24,587,217	240,878	23,514	588		do.
1915	9,217,622	90,661	12,016	300		do.
1916	10,334,793	93,980	17,896	447		do.
1917	7,481,468	69,128	43,870	227		do.
1918	14,680,823	137,649	20,640	212		do.
1919	10,432,250	103,238	nil.		7	210

NIGERIA, SOUTHERN PROVINCES

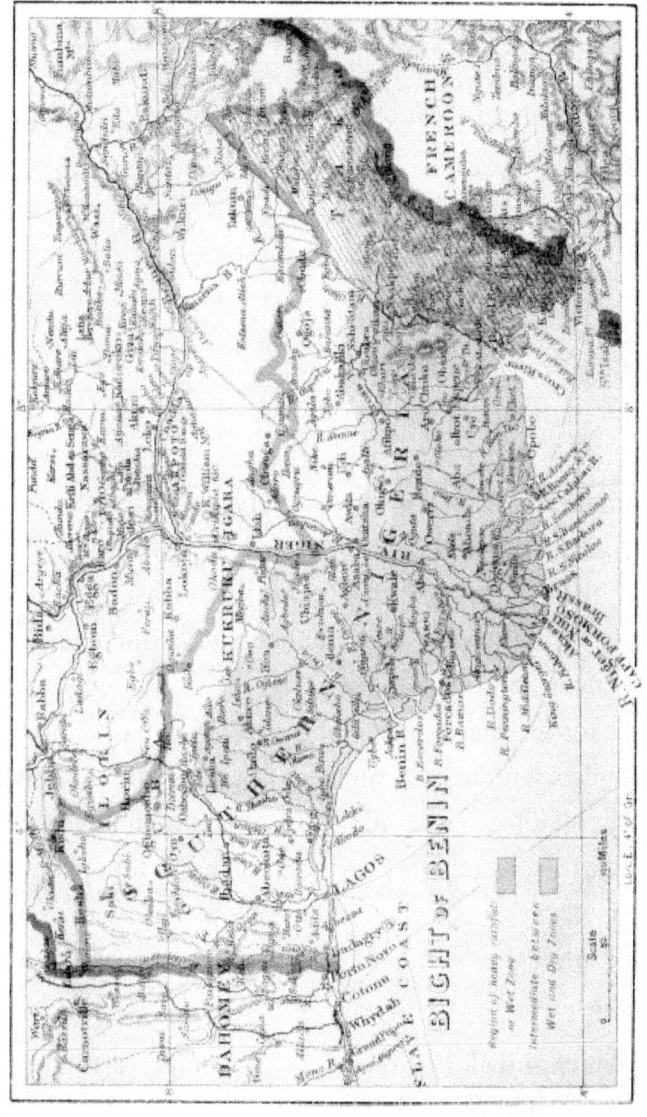

Stanford's Geogl. Estabt., London.

NIGERIA-SOUTHERN PROVINCES

INTRODUCTORY REMARKS. Administrative Divisions.—On January 1, 1914, the countries, hitherto administered separately under the names of Northern and Southern Nigeria, were amalgamated and placed under a Governor-General. It is, nevertheless, convenient, from the point of view of their agricultural and commercial interests, to deal with them in this place separately. The inhabitants of the Northern and Southern Provinces are to a very large extent dissimilar in languages, religion and customs, and the climatic conditions, by which distinct varieties of life are so much influenced, are so suitably defined by the artificial boundary which, until recently, divided Northern and Southern Nigeria, that little excuse need be offered for the maintenance of old division in the discussion of the subjects within the competence of this book. Following then the plan adopted in the first edition, Southern Nigeria, referred to now as the Southern Provinces, is being first dealt with and treated, as far as possible, independently of Northern Nigeria, now entitled the Northern Provinces, the separate account of which follows.

Geographical Position.—Pending the adjustment of the eastern frontier, occasioned by the outcome of the recent war, the Southern Provinces of Nigeria extend from 2° 45′ E. to 10°

15' E. long.: the Western Province reaching 9° 10' N., and the Central and Eastern about 7° 15' N. lat.

Area and Population.—The estimated area of the country before adjustment was 94,000 sq. miles, and the census of 1911 showed the population as 7,857,983.

Natural Divisions.—The Southern Provinces are conveniently divided for agricultural considerations into *wet* and *dry* zones. In the former the rainfall ranges from about 90 inches at Bendi to 250 inches at Opobo. In the latter zone the highest rainfall is reached in Lagos Town, where about 75 inches are annually registered; the lowest reading being that of 40 inches at Olokemeji. The densely forested area is practically entirely within the wet zone; this also including a tract of brackish-water forest (mangrove) and swamp. In the dry zone grass-land and open "bush," with trees peculiar to such localities, occur, and it is in this portion of the country that most of the agricultural people are found. The inhabitants of the forested area in the wet zone give more attention to the collection of forest products, such as palm oil and rubber, and only grow sufficient grain and roots for their own consumption.

Inhabitants.—The tribes found in the Western Province are chiefly Yorubas, and among these are some of the most intelligent people in the country. In the Central Province there are a large number of tribes speaking different languages, but among these the Benis are perhaps of most importance. The Ijoas, Ibos, Aros, and many other tribes inhabit the Eastern Province, and are generally of a lower grade of civilisation than the others mentioned. The country between the northern part of the Cross river and the Niger is populated by other pagan tribes, who seem to be careful cultivators, but very little is known of them at present.

Cultivation.—The Yoruba race are industrious cultivators, and show considerably more ambition than most of the other West African peoples. The country in which they live is particularly adapted to farming, and the climatic conditions are suitable for the cultivation of cotton and fibrous plants, in addition to the various grain crops. In some parts cocoa, rubber, and kola are being cultivated, but these are not so suitable under the prevailing conditions as they would be within the wet zone—the Western Province, which these people inhabit, being entirely within the dry region.

Although farming is so extensive, continuous cultivation is not found, and the use of manure is practically unknown. The usual practice is to farm a piece of land for a few years, and to permit it then to return to a wild state for a long period. In their want of knowledge concerning the value of manure and the application of artificial irrigation, the Yoruba farmers are behind the Haussas of Northern Nigeria, but are more careful than the Nupes of the same country. The depth of the Yoruba cultivation is greater than that of the northern Haussa, and this in some measure compensates for the non-employment of manure, etc.

The people of the Central Province are generally less careful in their farming methods; the Benis often planting their grain crops in only partially cleared land. Farther to the north in the same province a better system is noticeable among the Ishans, Ifons, and the people of Agbede. During recent years, owing to the energetic efforts of the Forestry Department, the cultivation and better treatment of the indigenous rubber tree (*Funtumia elastica*) have been extensively adopted, especially by the people in the neighbourhood of Benin City, where the climate is well suited to the species. In addition to rubber, cocoa and kola plantations might prove successful in the same localities, but as yet no large plantations of either exist.

In the Eastern Province farming is generally of poor quality until the region of heavy rainfall is left, when extremely large areas are met with, highly cultivated, with the earth thrown up into loose mounds, often five or six feet in height, for the purpose of growing yams, maize, pepper, okra, Guinea corn, pumpkins, etc., all of which are found planted upon each mound; the yams being carefully trained to climb along fibre strings towards central poles.

Principal Crops.—The chief crops grown in the Western Province are maize, cotton, cassava, yams, sweet potatoes, groundnuts, and to a small extent Guinea corn, sugar-cane, tobacco, Colocasia yams, peppers, okra, rice, eggplant, and native beans.

Indigo is extracted from *Lonchocarpus cyanescens*, which occurs in a wild state, and is preserved when making clearances for farms. The *Indigofera spp.* are used to a smaller degree for the same purpose. (See Sierra Leone Section, p. 39; also *Bulletin of the Imperial Institute*, 1909, p. 319; 1918, p. 11; and 1919, p. 31.)

Fruits are not grown plentifully, and are generally left in an uncultivated condition. The chief kinds are pineapples, bananas, pawpaws, akee apple (*Blighia sapida*), oranges, and guavas. There are several fruits and spices which are collected from the forest strips, but, taken generally, the Western Province people are not great fruit eaters. On the sea coast and for a considerable distance inland, coconut plantations are common, and, near Badagry, copra is prepared from them for shipment.

The crops cultivated in the Central Province are similar to those of the Western, but yams become more, and groundnuts less prominent. Large quantities of palm oil are prepared, and rubber is collected, the labour available for farm work being thereby reduced.

The most important product of the Eastern Province is undoubtedly palm oil, but fairly large quantities of yams and maize are grown outside the forest zone and are transported by native canoes to the coast ports, in the vicinity of which there is very little cultivation.

With the exception of the oil palm, which is of general occurrence throughout the country, the Lagos silk rubber tree (*Funtumia elastica*) is of the most importance from a commercial standpoint. Rubber vines of the genera *Landolphia* and *Carpodinus* are also valuable wild plants, from which some of the finest rubbers are at present extracted. Copal, known as "Ogea" gum, and collected from a tree which has been determined as *Cyanothyrsus oblongus* (syn. *ogea*), is exported in varying quantity according to the market value. A fairly extensive local trade is done in "chew-sticks" in the Western Province; the sticks being cut from a tree which occurs in the grass country, and is recognised as *Anogeissus leiocarpus*. The ash made from the wood of the same tree is sold for use as a mordant in indigo dyeing. Camwood is a red dye-wood prepared from at least three different species of trees—*Baphia nitida*, *Pterocarpus tinctorius*, and *Pterocarpus sp.*—and is almost entirely used locally for staining the human skin or dyeing leather. Fibre plants do not appear to be cultivated in any part of the country, but occur to some extent in all the forested parts. *Hibiscus guineensis* and *Dombeya buettneri* are usually employed for native ropes, and the bark of *Sterculia barteri* is said to be prepared for the same purpose.

OIL PALM.—A description of this tree and information in connection with the principal characteristics and mode of propagation have been given in the Sierra Leone portion of this work, and it may merely be remarked that there is no difference in a general way between trees grown in the two localities. With regard to the form of fruit, however, that of Southern Nigeria is separated into several kinds, varying in the relative proportion of pericarp and kernel, and these will be referred to later.

The method of preparing palm oil varies to a large degree in the different localities. The best quality of oil is that produced in the Western Province. The oil, which on the market is classed as "Lagos fine grade," and obtains the highest price among West African oils, is made from the fresh fruits boiled and pounded in the manner described for the Sierra Leone oil, but the extracted oil is further cleared by straining and boiling until a uniformly clear and limpid product is obtained.

STRAINING OIL FROM THE FIBROUS PULP OF THE OIL PALM,
OSHOGBO.
Fig. 22

COTTON BALES, MARLBOROUGH GINNERY, IBADAN.
Fig. 23

AFARA TREE (*TERMINALIA SUPERBA*) AT OLOKOMEJI.
Fig. 24

An inferior quality is that made at Oshogbo and north of Ibadan generally. The fruits, after having been boiled for about three hours, have the fibrous pulp sufficiently loosened, so that the whole is easily separated from the nuts by pounding in a wooden mortar. The fibrous mass thus obtained is then put into a pit, which is filled to a depth of about eighteen inches with cold water, and the oil is expressed by women and young girls, who tread it out with their feet. After leaving the water undisturbed for a short time, the oil rises to the surface, from which it is skimmed, or it may be precipitated, by the removal of a plug placed in the side of the pit, into a vessel placed to receive it. The treading process is repeated until most of the oil is extracted. The oil is then separated from the water which it contains by boiling. The fibrous pulp is next removed, strained in baskets, and is placed upon rocks to dry in the sun, after which it is pressed into large balls, which are sold in the local markets at 1d. each. Much of this finds its way to Lagos Town, where it is sold for fuel at the rate of 8d. for 8½ lb. In this connection it may be mentioned that there appears to be no foundation for the statement which has been made to the effect that this residual pulp is exported in large quantities from Lagos for the further extraction of oil by chemical means in Europe. An illustration is given showing a girl straining fibrous pulp in an oil pit at Oshogbo (Fig. 22).

In the Central and Eastern Provinces "hard" oil is the commercial name applied to the kind which is generally made. At Onitsha the natives may be seen bringing in this oil, which is of such a consistency that even at an atmospheric temperature of 90° it remains in a solid wax-like condition. The earthen vessels in which such oil is conveyed to the factories, when accidentally dropped and broken, do not necessarily occasion the loss of any oil. The thickened condition is entirely due to the method of preparation, during which important chemical changes occur, which appear to be detrimental to the oil for some of its most important uses, especially that of soap manufacture, while rendering it suitable for employment for making candles. The important difference in the preparation of this oil lies in the fact that instead of the fresh fruits being used, the pericarp is separated from the nuts by means of partial decomposition, induced by burying the fruits in the ground for a period varying from three weeks to two months. The semi-decomposed pericarp is then easily removed by pounding or treading out in a canoe-shaped receptacle, after which the fibrous mass is boiled, and the liquid oil is skimmed and allowed to set in earthen jars, in which it is carried for sale to the factories.

The extraction of kernels from the nuts is one of the usual occupations of the women and children of a village, when not assisting in the preparation of oil. The nuts are spread in the sun for about a week or more until a shrinkage of the kernel occurs, which renders the nut-shell capable of being easily cracked without damage to the interior. It is said that in the Jebu district, to the north-east of Lagos, the local price paid for kernels ranges from 4*d*. to 4½*d*. for a filled tin bowl having the diameter of nine inches.

The primitive method of extracting kernels, by means of cracking the nut-shell between stones and picking out the contents, has not yet given way to the employment of the various machines which have been introduced from time to time to supersede it.

A black oil is extracted at Oshogbo by roasting the kernels in an earthen pot until black, and stirring meanwhile until the whole mass becomes covered with exuded oil. A small quantity of cold water is then sprinkled into the pot after removing it from the fire, and the contents are pounded in a mortar until an oily meal is produced. This is boiled, and, when the mixture is cool, the oil is skimmed from the surface of the water which has been added for the boiling. This oil is apparently only used locally.

The existing native social system, under which the male head of a family receives almost exclusive consideration, is opposed to native co-operation in any mechanical process, whereby a relief from labour of his numerous dependants—wives, children, and aged or infirm relatives—would be incurred at the expense of his enhanced personal labour; he being the carrier and disposer of the produce at the market. By the conveyance and sale of nuts instead of kernels, a much smaller return in value would be obtained for the same weight of material, *i.e.* a similar amount of personal energy. The dependants, incapable of assisting in transporting, would remain idle, unless some similar work could be found for them. Up to a short distance from the delivery point (which would determine itself) the nuts instead of the kernels would be brought in for sale, and, limited by the capabilities of the available palm-tree climbers, the family dependants would be able to prepare larger quantities of pericarp oil; but the increased accumulation of kernels would further decrease the radius from the selling centre at which the carriers would be able to work.

If the entire fruit were to be bought up for mechanical extraction of pericarp oil as well as kernels, the carrying labour would be still further enhanced, and the work of the oil-manufacturing communities would resolve itself into three operations— viz. climbing trees, chopping out fruit, and transporting—which would mean the exclusion from work of all but the strong adults, or the reduction of workers by 30 to 50 per cent. perhaps. The number of skilled palm-tree climbers is said to be decreasing in many districts, and, owing to the sparsity of the population in some localities, a very large proportion of the annual yield of fruit remains unharvested.

The investigation of the several varieties of the oil palm of the country is in progress at the Imperial Institute, and the characters of the most important are now well known, and may be compared here with the varieties from the Gold Coast, Sierra Leone, Gambia, and Northern Nigeria. The typical form, which, although subject to some variation, possesses certain marked characteristics, may be said to fall under the following general description:

Fruiting heads generally large. Fruit large, orange to scarlet in colour, with a variable amount of purplish black suffusion at the apex, which may extend over more than half of the fruit or may be altogether absent. Pericarp thin, kernel large with a thick shell. Names: "Ope yope" or "Ope pankora" (Yoruba), "Ok-poruk-pu" (Ibo), "Udin" (Beni), "Ak-porro-jub" (Efik), "Irök-Eyop" (Ibibio), "Abe pa" and perhaps "Abe dam" (Fanti, Gold Coast), "Tug bore" (Mendi, Sierra Leone), "Tabel-tiloli" (Timani, Sierra Leone), "Tengo" (Mandingo, Gambia), "Kabe-kalako" (Jolah, Gambia), "Neul" (Joloff, Gambia), "Qua-qua" (Haussa, N. Nigeria), "Yi-ku-niche" (Nupe, N. Nigeria). Only the typical form has as yet been observed in Sierra Leone, Gambia, and Northern Nigeria.

The other particularly important variety is that commonly referred to as the "*soft-shelled*" or "*thin-shelled*" palm fruit, which has been recorded from many localities in West Africa.

The following description will include the forms contained in this group:

Fruiting heads often large. Fruits large or small, generally the latter, dark coloured. Pericarp thick, kernel rather small, with a thin shell. Names: "Ope-Arunfo" (Yoruba), "Au-su-ku" (Ibo), "Ivioronmila" (Beni), "Asoge-e-jub" (Efik), "Eduege Eyop" (Ibibio), "Abe-bobe" (Fanti, Gold Coast).

The third kind is that frequently called the "*Fetish*" or "*King*" palm nut. It is rare wherever it occurs, and is scarcely worth consideration from an economic standpoint. The tree which bears this fruit has been described under the distinct specific name of *Elæis Thompsoni*, Chevalier.

Fruiting heads generally small. Fruits medium-sized, red with black markings occasionally present. Pericarp moderately thick, kernel and shell medium. The nuts, which possess four eyes, are not used in the manufacture of commercial oil, but are employed in connection with the worship of the deity Ifa (Dennett). Names: "Ope Ifa" (Yoruba), "Ojuku" (Ibo), "Ogedudin" (Beni), "Affia-ko-jub" (Efik), "Efiako-Eyop" (Ibibio), "Abe-ohene" (Fanti, Gold Coast).

The above are the three most marked forms of oil palm recognisable, although other varieties are given special names by natives in different parts of the country, distinctions being frequently made between the fruit from trees which assume a tall growth and those which remain stunted. (Cf. also *Bull. Imp. Inst.*, 1909, p. 362; and 1920, p. 223.)

As far as investigations have progressed, the advantage with regard to yield of oil as well as quality is maintained by the thin-shelled variety, the greater proportion of pericarp enabling a larger amount of pericarp oil to be expressed, while the thin kernel-covering facilitates the extraction of the kernel. Before being able to definitely state that this variety is of the greatest economic value, it is necessary that a comparison of the weight of the annual crops from all varieties should be made.

The advisability of planting any particular variety of oil palm would in the first place depend on the results obtained from the complete investigation of all; but at the present time such a project on a large scale is not likely to be practicable, as it is generally acknowledged that only a comparatively small proportion of the existing wild trees are at present utilised.

Experiments in the Kamerun, with different varieties of oil palms, seemed to indicate that the thin-shelled character was not a fixed one. In 1910 a forest officer in Nigeria was detailed to study the distribution, cultivation and preparation of the oil, of the most appreciated varieties, and a quantity of nuts of the soft-shelled "Lisombe" kind from the Kamerun were distributed for planting among the natives of the Eastern Province.

The export figures of this trade from 1910 to 1918 are tabulated below. Up to the year 1914, those of Northern were separated from those of Southern Nigeria. In this account, subsequent to that year, the two sets of figures have been taken together. A quantity of kernels is imported from Dahomey for re-export, amounting in 1910 to 21,120 tons. The figures indicate that the increase has been irregular, and, during the last few years, has been influenced by the war. In 1919 here, as in the other W. African Colonies, a differential export tax of £2 per ton was imposed, with respect to palm kernels.

Year	Palm oil in tons (280 galls. = 1 ton)	Palm kernels in tons
1910	76,850	172,998
1911	79,337	176,390
1912	76,994	184,624
1913	83,088	174,718
1914	72,531	162,452
1915	72,994	153,319
1916	67,422	161,439
1917	74,619	185,998
1918	86,425	205,167
1919	100,967	216,913

It is interesting to compare the amount of oil produced in proportion to kernels collected, there being a marked difference in this respect between the output of the Western Province (Lagos) and the Central and Eastern Provinces. A previous series of thirteen years' exports from the former showed an average of 60·9 gallons of oil to the ton of kernels; while for the latter a twelve-year period at the same time gave 219·6 gallons of oil to the ton of kernels. The mean for the whole was 140·25 gallons at that time, but during the last seven years it has fallen to 125·7 gallons. In 1912 the first shipments of kernel oil and cake were made from factories established under European control at Opobo and Lagos, the amounts exported being 500 tons of oil and 635 tons of cake. In the following year the value of both products turned out by these factories is given as £161,000, and in 1914 as £72,000, when, without any assigned reason, both factories were closed down.

Articles on the African palm-oil industry in the Southern

Provinces of Nigeria will be found in *Bulletin of the Imperial Institute*, 1909, 1911, 1912, 1913, 1914, 1915, 1919.

An interesting article appears in the *Bulletin of the Imperial Institute*, vol. xviii., No. 2 (1920), entitled "The Cultivation of the African Oil Palm, with special reference to the East Indies." From this it appears that the tree thrives and yields very satisfactorily, especially in Sumatra; the oil content of the fruit and kernels being both high. Attention is drawn in this article to the extension of the use of palm oil in Europe as an edible fat, in addition to its present uses.

Other Oil Seeds.—Excluding the shea nut tree, which will be referred to later on, three trees have been considered of sufficient importance for their seeds to be shipped to Europe in order that their value may be determined. These are *Pentaclethra macrophylla* (Cutlass bean), *Irvingia Barteri* (African mango), and *Lophira alata*. Although the trials proved that the oils of all might be valuable for the manufacture of soap and candles, none of the trees occur in sufficient profusion to permit a large export trade in the seeds being established. (See *Bulletin of the Imperial Institute*, vol. v. [1907], pp. 10-14, and vol. vi. [1908], pp. 243, 354-80.)

RUBBER.—Following the progress made by the Forestry Department in re-establishing the indigenous rubber tree (*Funtumia elastica*) in places from which it had almost disappeared, an excellent system of communal plantations was established. This system, which has been largely adopted by the chiefs, is one to encourage the village inhabitants to re-establish rubber trees in their proximity; the planting and tapping and preparation of the rubber being under the direction of the Government officers. The resulting rubber is marketed by the

Government, who retain one-third of the sale price to cover the cost of supervision, etc.; the remaining two-thirds being paid to the village community. In this manner a large number of communal plantations have now been established. In 1911 over 400 new plantations of this kind were made; about 100,000 Funtumia plants being put in. At the same time 129,000 Para rubber seeds and some 4,000 seedlings were distributed under the same scheme, while Ceara plantations were made in the drier parts of the country. Licences to collect wild rubber were simultaneously made compulsory.

The rubber produced on the Government plantation at Mamu Forest, by the boiling method, proved very satisfactory. In 1910 such rubber was sold at 6s. 6d. per lb., being only 6d. less than the best Para fetched at the same time. Three hundred communal plantations yielded rubber in 1911 against eighty-four in the previous year, the average yield per tree being 1·59 oz. against 1·406 oz. In 1912 communal rubber amounted to 3,031 lbs., which sold at about 3s. 4d. per lb.; and in the same year Government plantation rubber was 3,501 lbs., which realised 3s. 10d. per lb.

The next rubber plant of importance is the vine, *Landolphia owariensis*, which is somewhat variable in the form of growth. The latex at certain seasons coagulates almost instantaneously, but at other times it runs freely, and can be collected for coagulation by heat, the admixture of acid, alkali or alcohol, or by spontaneous exposure. The scrap rubber, which is collected from that coagulated upon the stem, is made into balls, and comes into the market under the name of "first Niggers," and commands a high price.

The native has discovered that a larger amount of rubber

can be obtained at one time if the roots and stems are cut and pounded up. The result is a product known as "root rubber," the collection of which can be justified only where the plant, from which it is obtained, develops an extensive rhizome or subterranean growth, capable of being partially removed without killing the plant. Such vines, although found in some other parts of Africa, do not occur in Southern Nigeria, and the collection of so-called "root rubber" from *L. owariensis* only leads to the complete destruction of the plant, and should be discouraged. The small yield of latex from this species after many years of growth, and the difficulties in connection with the collection of the rubber, render its cultivation in plantations unprofitable, although planting has been attempted in the French and German Colonies.

Clitandra elastica is another vine said to yield a copious supply of latex, capable of being coagulated by means of heating after dilution with water. In appearance the vine is somewhat similar to *L. owariensis*, but does not appear to be common. The rubber produced from this species is reported to be of excellent quality.

Carpodinus hirsutus, a common vine in the dry zone and on the Niger river banks, furnishes a plentiful supply of latex of inferior quality, and is made into "root" and "paste" rubber by boiling; the latter being a sticky product of the consistency of birdlime, and only saleable in Europe at a low price.

The latices of *Landolphia Thompsonii* and *L. senegalensis* are used similarly. Both species are nearly allied to *L. florida*, which is prepared elsewhere.

A number of latex-yielding plants are employed in the adulteration of good rubber, among which the following may be mentioned as the commonest: *Funtumia africana*, *Conopharyngia sp.*, *Alstonia congoensis*, and *Holarrhena Wulfsburgii*. The admixture of these is usually detected by the stickiness which they impart to good rubber.

The introduction of licences for permission to collect wild rubber and that of the communal plantation system, previously referred to, have rendered the position more secure than previously, and insured the preservation of the wild plants which were threatened with extinction. This has moreover been effected in the most economical manner.

The results of the tappings on the Para rubber plantations in different parts of the country are of interest. In 1911 at Ebute Metta, trees eighteen years old yielded 3 lbs. 5½ oz. per tree; at Calabar six year old trees gave an average of 6 oz. per tree; while at Sapele in the same year, five year old trees yielded from 14 oz. to 1 lb. 6½ oz. per tree. In the following year the same trees at Ebute Metta gave 7 lbs. 4¾ oz., while those at Sapele yielded from 1 lb. 4¾ oz. to 1 lb. 11¾ oz. In 1915 from two Para rubber estates at Sapele 94,413 lbs. of dry rubber was harvested. (Cf. *Bull. Imp. Inst.*, 1910, 1912, 1913, 1918.)

Export of Rubber.—The Commercial Intelligence Officer of Southern Nigeria, in his report on the trade of the country for 1907, gives a table showing the rubber exported from Southern Nigerian ports from 1900 to 1907; but as these figures include large quantities of the product from Northern Nigeria, shipped through Southern Nigerian ports, they do not represent the output from the latter country alone. Until 1907 apparently no record of the Northern Nigerian rubber exported was kept, but in the year mentioned 1,187,588 lbs., valued at £91,074, were recorded as having passed the customs post of Northern Nigeria at Ida, on the Niger. The amounts, in tons, exported from the Southern Provinces alone were: 1907, 690; 1908, 545; 1909, 620; and from the whole of Nigeria from that time: 1910, 1,180; 1911, 966; 1912, 705; 1913, 510; 1914, no figures; 1915, 248; 1916, 396; 1917, 392; 1918, 157; 1919, 398. The rubber production of the country is to some extent controlled by the market price, which is at present very low (1921).

COPAL.—Some quantity of a kind of copal resin is collected from *Cyanothyrsus oblongus* (syn. *C. ogea*), and is exported under the name of "Ogea gum." The quality appears to be similar to that obtained from the Gold Coast *Cyanothyrsus sp.*, and which is sold under the name of "Accra copal." Both are obtained in a fresh and a fossil state. Owing to the recent fall in the price of ogea gum, the collection of it has diminished, but there are said to be large quantities available which would be collected as soon as a better demand occurred. (See articles on "Copal Resins from British West Africa," *Bull. Imp. Inst.*, 1908, p. 245; and 1914, p. 218.)

COCOA.—The good fortune which has recently attended the planters in West Africa, owing to a sudden demand for their cocoa, has encouraged them, especially to the north and north-east of Lagos, to make more extensive plantations. The climatic conditions in the Western Province, however, are not favourable, and the repeated failures of trees, due to the exhausting effect of the long dry seasons, give the plantations an irregular appearance. The trees in the plantations made at Agege, where many well-to-do planters have made farms, are stunted, and planted in too close proximity, mostly without permanent shade trees. In some instances the trees showed disease from the sapping of the bark juices occasioned by a Capsid, the species of which is as yet undetermined. The chief cause of their sterility and death seems, however, to be the unfavourable climatic conditions. In the direction of the Abeokuta-Ibadan boundary, better planting seems to have been done and permanent shade trees preserved.

It is said that the Agege planters are dissatisfied with the prices they obtain for their cocoa, which they maintain is properly fermented and of better quality than that of their neighbours. An association of the local planters was recently formed to ship their own produce direct to the European markets. The Agege cocoa generally, however, does not appear to be more carefully prepared or of better quality than the other local kinds. Fermentation is certainly practised in many places, and is becoming popular throughout the Western Province, owing to the discovery that the fermented pulp juice forms a beverage, which is said to be used as a substitute for palm wine, but the beans are frequently improperly dried.

In the Eastern Province the climatic conditions appear to be more favourable for the plant, and there are now a number of small plantations near Eket, Old Calabar, and Itu. The product is still improperly prepared and usually unfermented, but time and experience will remedy this.

In the Central Province from 1915 some activity in cocoa planting has occurred in the Benin district, but attention there is still mainly devoted to rubber planting.

See also *Bull. Imp. Inst.*, 1914, p. 213; 1915, p. 553; and 1919, p. 289.

The exports of cocoa have been as follows:

Year	Lagos (W. Province) lbs.	value £	S. Nigeria (C. & E. Provs.) lbs.	value £
1890	13,657	322	No record	
1891	15,254	332	,,	
1892	15,820	390	,,	
1893	18,027	488	46,977	655
1894	39,177	929	58,180	992
1895	48,187	832		1,520
1896	27,968	442	109,399	1,532
1897	101,186	1,528	101,214	1,393
1898	76,965	1,579	120,633	1,459
1899	157,708	3,411	142,235	2,548
1900	256,234	5,913	196,455	2,710
1901	229,952	5,042	230,726	3,139
1902	385,540	7,530	302,305	3,677
1903	341,461	6,705	288,614	3,653
1904	821,732	13,892	367,728	4,982
1905	896,350	10,889	388,479	6,019
1906	1,153,439	20,893	466,548	6,161
1907	Combined		2,089,225	47,840
1908	,,		3,060,609	50,587
1909	,,		5,019,417	71,917
1910	,,		6,567,181	101,150
1911	,,		9,858,774	164,664
1912	,,		7,593,711	130,542
1913	,,		8,111,920	157,480

1914	„	5,000	tons app.	171,751
1915	„	9,105	„	313,946
1916	„	8,956	„	393,101
1917	„	15,442	„	499,009
1918	„	10,219	„	235,870
1919	„	25,711	„	1,067,675

COTTON.—Reviewing the work which has been done in inducing the agricultural population of the country to cultivate cotton for export, by far the greatest prominence must be given to the untiring efforts of the British Cotton Growing Association, who are gradually surmounting all the obstacles which retarded their progress. The condition of the industry, especially in the Western Province, is extremely favourable, and shows signs of further development.

In every Yoruba market sales of cotton are now conducted as a part of the regular transactions of the day, and cotton from distant villages filters through from market to market, increasing in value as it approaches a ginnery, where the full price for it may be ultimately claimed by the trader who has collected it.

On account of this system of passing from one market to another, chiefly in the form of barter for other produce, it becomes nearly impossible to accurately determine the origin of the supplies brought to the ginneries; and, by reference to the records kept, very large quantities of cotton often appear as having been sent from towns which are little more than accumulating centres, and in the vicinity of which there is little or no cotton grown.

Experience in the plantation of cotton under European

control has shown that without combining the work of a general trader, farmer, and ginner with that of grower, such an attempt is not likely to prove remunerative. The British Cotton Growing Association have abandoned development upon these lines, directing their attention solely towards buying, ginning and inducing the native farmers to cultivate the plant in their ordinary field rotations. Such plantations as still exist are now under the direct control of the Government and are maintained for the purpose of experimental work and for the propagation of improved types.

The local varieties of cotton may be roughly classed under five heads, which are easily recognisable by the characters of the seed and lint. These are:

1. Black, clean-seeded with a brown tuft or brown woolly and a brick-red lint.—"Eponkon."

2. Black, clean-seeded, with a creamy white lint.—Common Western Province kind; rarer in the Central Province (Ishan).

3. Black, adhering seeds, "kidney" kind, lint creamy.—Common Central Province.

4. White or brownish woolly seeded, lint creamy.—Meko and Agbede kinds.

5. Green woolly seeded, lint creamy.—Rather uncommon except at Agege.

The characters of the above classes do not appear to be sufficiently constant to render it easy to give each class a specific position, although some of them are doubtless separable. All native forms of plant are constantly of greater stature than American, and in this particular resemble Egyptian kinds.

The red-linted form known as "Eponkon" is identical with

the "Dhoole" of Sierra Leone, and, although prolific, yields a cotton which is of little value for export. The other four kinds are those from which the Southern Nigerian output of exported cotton is almost wholly obtained, and the price realised varies from ½d. under to 1d. or more over Middling American. The finest cottons are those grown at Agege and Meko; the former being supposed to be a hybrid with an American variety, and the latter a constant local variety. Some of the shipments, from Illushi, of cotton grown near Agbede appear to have been of equally desirable quality.

A large number of specimens of cotton have been examined at the Imperial Institute, and the length of fibre is generally found to be over one inch in average, but the colour is yellowish, and there is less lustre than is found in the American kinds. Although the price obtained is often somewhat higher than that of the standard Middling American grade, Manchester spinners do not regard West African cotton as quite suitable for their ordinary requirements, and it appears that the higher prices have only been paid for small quantities which were capable of being used for special purposes.

For the reason mentioned, efforts have been made to replace the indigenous cottons by American kinds, or to hybridise the two, but the results have not yet been successful, the tendency being to produce an irregular mixed lint, which is commercially inferior. American and Egyptian cottons seem to be less capable of withstanding the attacks of the local insect pests, and a large proportion of the seed is rendered sterile by the cotton seed bug. Grown experimentally on a small scale at Olokemeji, the following results were obtained from several exotic and local cottons (American Middling at 6·64d. per lb.):—

	Variety	Yield per A.	lbs. Lint %	Staple average	Value
1.	Black Rattler	82·5	36·36	1·3 in.	6⅝—6¾d.
2.	Richmond	140	28·5	1·1 ,,	6⅝-6¾d.
3.	Eponkon	525	24·7	1·2 ,,	no demand
4.	Abassi	210	31	1·5 ,,	7⅛d.
5.	Ashmouni	300	33·3	1·3 ,,	6¾d.
6.	Jannovitch	120	33·3	1·0 ,,	6⅝-6¾d.
7.	Kidney	340	41	1·2 ,,	6¾d.
8.	Georgia	150	36·6	1·1 ,,	6⅝-6¾d.
9.	Ogudu	490	28·5	1·5 ,,	7d.
10.	Sea Island	60	33·3	1·4 ,,	6¾d.
11.	Allen's Improved	195	30·7	1·6 ,,	7⅛d.
12.	Culpepper B. Boll.	150	33·3	1·2 ,,	6⅝-6¾d.
13.	Jannovitch	240	33·3	1·5 ,,	7d.
14.	Peruvian	400	17·5	1·2 ,,	6-6¾d.
15.	Abassi	320	34·4	1·4 ,,	7½d.
16.	Jones' improved	82·5	36·36	1·4 ,,	6d.
17.	Russell's B.B.	Crop entire failure			
18.	Hawkins' Extra Prolific	,, ,, ,,			
19.	Sunflower Box Staple	,, ,, ,,			

Of the above Nos. 1, 2, 8, 10, 11, 12, 14, 16, 17, 18, and 19 are American varieties, and were grown from seed supplied by the British Cotton Growing Association; Nos. 4, 5, 6, 13 and 15 are Egyptian; No. 9 is a Northern Nigerian variety from North Ilorin, and Nos. 3 and 7 appear to be local kinds. These cottons are referred to in Professor Dunstan's Report (1907), "British Cotton Cultivation."

In addition to the susceptibility of the American varieties to the attacks of the local insect pests, the seed produced from plants grown in the country is often sterile. In the districts in the vicinity of the British Cotton Growing Association's ginneries American and native cottons are often seen growing in the same field, but as the time of reaching maturity differs in the various forms, and the cotton is not easily kept separate in the native methods of harvesting, a mixed crop is obtained. Experimenting at the Moor Plantation at Ibadan, the British Cotton Growing Association have obtained occasionally satisfactory results from the American plots, as appeared to be the case in the 1908-9 season, when an American "Upland" variety is said to have yielded 800 lbs. of seed cotton per acre. In the previous year an indigenous variety called "Meko" is recorded as having produced over 900 lbs. to the acre. These results are largely dependent upon the season and the time of sowing.

Artificial pollination of the female flowers of the local forms with pollen taken from American kinds has not yet succeeded in producing a permanent hybrid, although the result in the first generation has frequently shown great promise. There is no doubt that the establishment of a hybrid which would carry the lint of the best American kind and retain the hardiness and blight-resisting powers of the indigenous forms would be very desirable, but such a type could only be evolved after careful experiment and selection for a prolonged period. Such work may probably be undertaken by the Agricultural Department in the future. Until this can be scientifically taken up, the improvement of the existing forms by a more gradual means should be attempted, namely by a careful selection of seed and elimination of undesirable forms of plants in the field.

Where cotton is planted by natives, the cultivation is usually carefully carried out. Planting takes place in June, July, or August, and the crop is harvested from January until April. For the most part cotton is grown by the Yorubas as a separate crop, although occasionally it may be found in conjunction with maize. No manuring is carried on, but the crops are generally fair, except in the proximity of the Niger, for an unexplained reason. No estimate can be made of the yield per acre from native cotton fields, but from 60 to 80 bolls are frequently found upon a single plant.

Before passing to other matters in connection with the condition of the cotton plant in the country, and the appliances in use for the preparation of the lint for export, it seems advisable to emphasise the main points which require attention in the field. 1. Improvement of the indigenous forms, by the careful selection of seed at the ginneries, for distribution, and the subsequent elimination of undesirable types of plant in the field. 2. Demonstration to the native farmer of a useful method of combination of cotton with the existing field crops, and especially the advantage of introducing leguminous crops into the rotation with cotton. 3. Special efforts to be made in those countries outside the oil palm districts, where the natives have little else capable of being produced for barter for imported material. Alter a series of experimental trials it was decided in 1915 to encourage the planting of Georgia cotton in the Western Province. In the year mentioned this American variety had yielded 800 lbs. of seed cotton per acre at Ibadan.

A number of insect pests of a more or less serious nature attack the plant at different periods of growth. The American boll-worm (*Chloridea obsoleta*) does some damage annually in the Central Province (Ugboha, Agbede and Ishan); *Earias insulana*, F., the Egyptian boll-worm; *E. imbricata*, an allied species, and *Diparopsis castanea* Hamp., the Sudan boll-worm, are common at Ibadan. The immature boll is often punctured by a scarlet and brown bug, identified as *Dysdercus superstitiosus*, Fabr., which enters the opened bolls also, and exudes a yellowish liquid, which stains the lint. The opened boll is also infested with three species of cotton-seed bugs—*Oxycarenus hyalinipennis*, *O. gossipinus*, and *O. Dudgeoni*—which do a large amount of damage in sapping the juices from the seed and rendering it unproductive. The most satisfactory method of dispersing this insect is to place the seed-cotton in a hot sun for several hours. Both *Oxycarenus* and *Dysdercus* may be trapped by placing piles of seed in the field at intervals, and treating them with kerosene when the insects have collected on them. A small caterpillar belonging to the family *Gelechiadœ*[4] is often found in the boll feeding on the seed, and a leaf-blistering blight, probably *Chlorita flavescens*, appears to be common in several places. A malady, chiefly on stems of exotic cottons, and known as "black-arm" in Georgia, U.S.A., is seen occasionally. The affection is not attributed to any animal or vegetable parasite.

The ginneries erected by the British Cotton Growing Association are probably some of the best equipped in the world. The Marlborough Ginnery at Ibadan (Fig. 23) has at present the largest output, although the Jones Ginnery at Oshogbo is larger, and is expected to receive a greater quantity of cotton for treatment in the future. The third, which is working in the Western Province, is the Churchill Ginnery at Lafenwa, near Abeokuta. Smaller ginneries have been erected at Eruwa Road, Iwo, Oyo, and Agege in the Western Province, but are at present unused. In the Central Province the Illushi Ginnery on the Niger is capable of treating all the cotton of the adjoining districts. A photograph of cotton bales at Ibadan is reproduced (Fig. 23).

At Ibadan an oil mill has been erected in connection with the Marlborough Ginnery, and the expression of oil from the seed is regularly carried on. The seed cake which is turned out is found to be of rather inferior quality for European consumption, as the excess of woolly seed renders it undesirable for cattle food. A very economical local use for this cake has recently been discovered—namely the employment of it to generate gas to drive the machinery of the ginnery. It has been found that 6 cwt. of cotton-seed cake is sufficient to generate gas to drive the 30 h.p. oil-mill engine for nine and a half hours. This discovery suggests the possibility of doing without coal entirely at the ginneries, which would mean a very large saving in the cost of production of cotton.

The cotton ginned by the British Cotton Growing Association is baled for the most part in rectangular oblong form, each bale weighing approximately 400 lbs. The production of the country has shown a rapid increase, especially in the earlier years, though more recently one of the seasons proved a short one owing to adverse climatic conditions.

	Weight cwts.		Weight cwts.		Weight cwts.
1902	110	1908	20,485	1914	no figure given
1903	2,588	1909	44,937	1915	24,081
1904	10,255	1910	22,128	1916	66,555
1905	12,275	1911	19,984	1917	47,137
1906	24,071	1912	39,043	1918	13,214
1907	36,513	1913	56,796	1919	60,221

The exports of cotton-seed in 1912 and 1913 reached 4,058 tons and 5,887 tons respectively. ("Cotton Varieties," cf. *Bull. Imp. Inst.*, vol. xv. [1917]). Much is expected from this new development.

MAIZE.—In the last few years the cultivation of a short-season "white" maize has been taken up, especially among the Yorubas, in the Western Province, although the variety is also found in the fields farther to the east. (See *Bulletin of the Imperial Institute*, vol. vii. [1909], pp. 145-8.)

	Tons	Value £		Tons	Value £
1907	9,891	28,520	1913	11,841	40,349
1908	15,529	51,695	1914	—	5,803
1909	10,917	34,335	1915	272	941
1910	5,096	16,689	1916	981	5,064
1911	867	3,128	1917	876	4,367
1912	7,899	28,713	1918	405	3,696

A difficulty has arisen in connection with the preparation of the crop for shipment; it having been found that very large quantities arrive in Europe in a weevilly condition. Various methods have been suggested to remedy this, including disinfection with carbon bisulphide, but the use of this last is dangerous.

A restriction with regard to the time of buying the July—August crop is recommended for adoption by the merchants, in order to prevent immature, insufficiently dried corn being shipped. It is insisted, however, in some quarters, that, until the holds of ships are systematically cleaned out before loading, no amount of precaution on shore will prevent shipments becoming weevilled during the voyage. (See article on "The Cultivation and Marketing of Maize" in the *Bulletin of the Imperial Institute*, vol. vi. [1908], pp. 261-77.)

Experiments were carried out in 1911, 1912 and 1913 to determine the most profitable time for sowing maize. The results were, however, conflicting, and no definite recommendation could be made owing to the irregularity of rainfall.

CASSAVA.—Among the more important field crops, cassava has to be reckoned. Two well-marked forms occur, which are readily recognised by the different characters of their leaves, one having the leaflets digitate and pointed, and the other digitate and spathulate, with the central leaflet shortened. Cassava forms an important food in many parts of the country, and is widely cultivated, especially in the Western Province. No tapioca is prepared from the root in Southern Nigeria, such as is the case in the West Indies and elsewhere.

YAMS.—In many parts of the country, more especially in the Central and Eastern Provinces, the various forms of yam (*Dioscorea*) are extensively cultivated alone or with maize, but the presence of five or six other crops growing upon the heightened yam mounds is not uncommon, in the Cross River districts particularly. From the latter locality quantities of yams are sent by river canoes to the large ports in the vicinity of which cultivated land is often scarce.

The Koko yam (*Colocasia antiquorum*) is also common in the wet zone.

GROUNDNUTS.—The cultivation of groundnuts (*Arachis hypogea*), upon a more extensive scale than at present, is to be recommended, as there are too few leguminous crops grown in the local rotation. The colour of most of the Southern Nigerian nuts is probably an obstacle to their ready sale in Europe; the shell being usually a dirty greyish instead of a light straw colour. The kernels are, however, satisfactory. It would, perhaps, therefore be advantageous to ship decorticated nuts, as is done in the Northern Provinces. Although new seed and instructors have been brought recently from the Gambia, very little more is grown than formerly.

The variety seen in the Western Province is a larger one than that of the Gambia, and has generally two kernels. The market price for groundnuts at Lapita near Oyo was 200 for 1d., which will indicate the scarcity of the product.

SHEA NUTS AND BUTTER.—The export trade in shea nuts (*Butyrospermum Parkii*) was expected to develop with the extension of the railway through Ibadan and Ilorin to the Northern Provinces, but the exported product still has its main source from localities north of the Niger. The demand does not seem sufficient to induce expansion to a great extent (*Bull. Imp. Inst.*, vol. vi. [1908]).

The butter or fat is much appreciated in the country for culinary purposes, and has been found of value in Europe for soap and candle-making, as well as for the manufacture of vegetable butter.

KOLA.—Two species of kola (*K. acuminata* and *K. vera*) are cultivated, the latter being the indigenous Gold Coast form, the fruit of which is said to be especially valued in the Haussa countries to the north. The local native names are, respectively, "Obi abatta" and "Obi gbanja." In general appearance the trees are similar, except that the former has narrower and smaller leaves. The "gbanja" form of nut is generally pink and divisible into from two to three parts (cotyledons), whereas the "abatta" form may vary in colour from deep crimson to white and be separable into from three to five parts. The price paid for kolas in Lagos is said to vary from 1*s*. 3*d*. to 5*s*. per hundred.

Although a considerable number of trees have been planted and are bearing fruit in the Western Province, the demand for kolas for native consumption is so great that there is a large import trade from the Gold Coast.

The kola nut is chewed in much the same manner as the betel nut in the East. It is greatly appreciated for its sustaining qualities, and forms a token of friendship exchanged among high-grade natives, as a preliminary to an important discussion of any kind.

FIBRE.—Experiments have been made at the Olokemeji Botanic Station with indigenous fibres, and a small factory has been erected at Ilaro, where a machine capable of extracting fibre is said to have been instituted. The reports upon some of the local Hibiscus fibres have been satisfactory. These are capable of utilisation as jute substitutes, and it may be possible to grow them in the crop rotation of the country at some future time for the purpose of export. (See *Selected Reports from the Imperial Institute*, No. 1 "Fibres," pp. 38, 52, 83, 89, and 114.)

Piassava (*Raphia vinifera*) fibre is prepared and shipped, especially from Uwet in the Eastern Province, the export amounting to 319 tons in 1910.

LEATHER.—A small trade in leather is done among the Yorubas, and tanners may be met with chiefly in the north of the Western Province. The process employed in the preparation of the goat and sheep skins used is similar to that of Northern Nigeria. (See Report on "Leather from Lagos," *Bulletin of the Imperial Institute*, vol. iv. [1906], p. 366, and articles on "Native

Leather of West Africa," *Bulletin of the Imperial Institute*, vol. vi. [1908], pp. 175-81 and vol. viii. [1910], pp. 402.)

TOBACCO.—Tobacco is produced near Ibadan, and large quantities are sold in the King's market of that town. It is probable that the curing of the leaf is done completely in the sun, as the prepared material is of a rather light colour and has a mild flavour. The leaves are apparently rather mixed, and old or immature examples are frequently included in the same grade.

Experiments will be taken in hand with a view to the improvement of the quality, but at present the local demand is so great that there is little prospect of an export trade becoming established. Recent work in Nyasa-land has shown that good pipe smoking tobacco, suitable for consumption in England, can be produced in Africa.

SILK.—The preparation of a silk yarn, carded and spun from the boiled cocoons of wild silkworms, is a common occupation of some of the women of Ibadan. The identity of the insects producing the silk has been determined to be *Anaphe infracta* and *A. venata*, both of which form congregated masses of cocoons. The yarn is of a brown colour, and is woven with cotton into a cloth which is called locally "Sanyan." It is much valued by the natives on account of its durability. The silkworms show some sign of becoming scarce owing to the utilisation of the pupæ as food. (See *Bulletin of the Imperial Institute*, 1910, p. 150; 1916, p. 168; and 1920, p. 319.)

COCONUTS.—The preparation of copra is carried on at Badagri, where a large coconut plantation exists. Great alarm was recently caused to the proprietors through the attack of a scale insect (*Aspidiotus destructor*), which destroyed the leaves of a very large number of trees. The advent of this pest was, however, quickly followed by the vast multiplication of the numbers of a species of large ladybird beetle, which soon checked the spread of the scale. The directions issued by the Forestry Department with regard to the means of destroying the infected leaves also assisted in the extermination of the blight.

MAHOGANY AND EBONY.—Among the valuable exported products from the country, mahogany and ebony must be regarded as occupying an important place. The largest proportion of the timbers exported to Europe and sold under the name of mahogany are obtained in the Central Province, and are cut from trees belonging to the genera *Khaya*, *Pseudocedrela*, and *Entandrophragma*, of the Natural Order *Meliaceæ*. Mr. Thompson, Conservator of Forests, remarks that a fair number of logs cut from a species of *Guarea*, of the same Natural Order, have been shipped, and have obtained good prices in Europe.

A red wood, called locally "Iroko" (*Chlorophora excelsa*), which is in good demand in the country for making furniture, etc., has been shipped to Europe, but at present there is little demand for it. A photograph of another timber tree (*Terminalia superba*) is given (Fig. 24).

Mahogany cannot be relied upon as a product capable of permanent exportation, as trees are only useful for felling in the vicinity of creeks and rivers, whence the logs may be inexpensively transported to the sea. The rate at which the available trees are becoming worked out is much greater than that at which they can be replaced by nature.

The export values for some recent years are as under:—

| 1910 | £60,191 | 1915 | £54,559 |
| 1911 | £55,575 | 1916 | £49,361 |

1912	£78,007		1917	£21,282
1913	£105,440		1918	£68,480
1914	£86,522		1919	£116,820

The ebony exported from the country is chiefly obtained in the Cross River District of the Eastern Province, but during recent years the trade in it has diminished, and it is said that immature trees are frequently felled. The sources of ebony are two species of trees belonging to the genus *Diospyros*. The value of ebony exported during the two years 1909 and 1910 is stated to have been £1,298 and £166 respectively.

Several other trees have recently been examined for export value, most of them coming into the mahogany or red-wood class. (See articles on "Timbers from Southern Nigeria," *Bull. Imp. Inst.*, vol. vi. [1908], p. 144, vol. xviii. [1920], p. 199, and note on next page.)

CATTLE.—The greater part of the moist zone is almost devoid of cattle, partly owing to the prevalence of "tsetse" fly, although mainly, perhaps, to the less advanced condition of the inhabitants. As soon as the intermediate and dry-zone country is entered, small herds are frequently seen. That the presence of tsetse fly is not entirely accountable for the scarcity of cattle in the forested region is shown by the occurrence of the peculiar dwarfed variety with short legs, which is found in Ondo, Ilesha, Ifon, Ishan, and even in the Bassa Province in Northern Nigeria, in all of which districts "tsetse" flies of at least two species are met with. (*Glossina palpalis* and *G. pallidipes*.) It is stated by the natives that the dwarf cattle are immune from fly disease, but that introduced animals succumb to it. The appearance of these animals, an illustration of one of which is given, reproduced from a photograph taken at Illara (Fig. 25), is remarkable. The prevailing colours are black and white, black, and more rarely fawn-coloured. There is no dorsal hump, and the forequarters are generally lower than the hind. A second illustration, from a photograph taken at Owo (Fig. 26), gives an idea of the relative size of a full-grown animal compared with that of a boy. Another peculiarity of the above-mentioned districts is that the goats occurring there are similarly short-legged and diminutive; there is also said to be a stunted variety of horse, which is bred for use at Ondo. When the open country is reached, two varieties of cattle are seen, one of the Indian zebu type, with a large dorsal hump, the prevailing colour of which is white, and another with a straight back. The latter kind is seen as far south as Onitsha, on the east bank of the Niger.

DWARF CATTLE, ILLARA.
Fig. 25

OWO.
Fig. 26

HAUSSA CULTIVATING IMPLEMENTS (LEFT TO RIGHT: I. FATAIN-YA, II. GARMA, III. SANGUMI), NORTHERN PROVINCES.
Fig. 27

POTTERY.—Earthen pots are made in several parts of the country, and are usually symmetrically formed, although no wheel is used in their preparation. The large earthen jars made at Abeokuta are used in the palm oil, native beer, and indigo industries.

FOREST RESERVES.—These are now being formed everywhere in order to replace the destruction of recent years. The irregular rainfall renders natural regeneration very poor, and artificial regeneration by means of planting by leaseholders for trees cut down has proved unsatisfactory. In 1913 some villages in the Central Province started small mahogany plantations, and trees for fuel are now being grown in several districts. The value of such trees as *Afzelia africana* and *Triplochiton johnsoni* has been recently demonstrated.

NIGERIA, NORTHERN PROVINCES

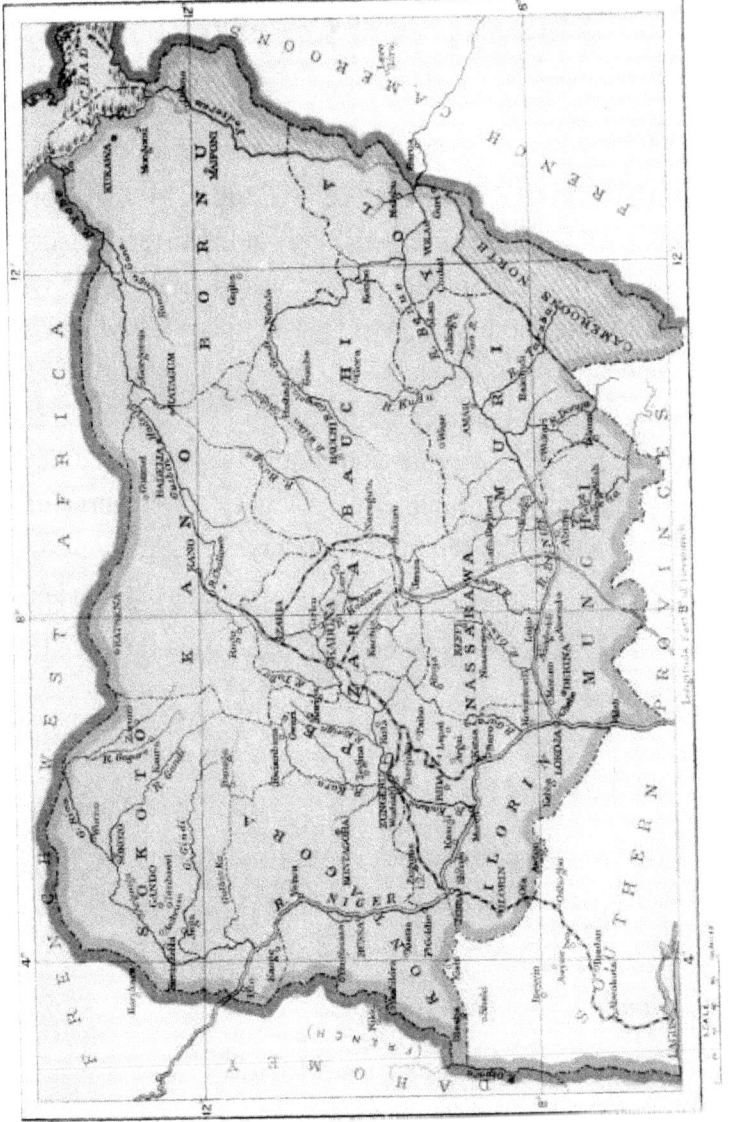

Stanford's Geogl. Estabt., London.

NIGERIA-NORTHERN PROVINCES

INTRODUCTORY REMARKS—Until 1914 the Northern Provinces of Nigeria were separately administered under the designation of Northern Nigeria, and were the largest as well as the most recent of our West African Colonies. They lie between 7° 3' and 13° 54' north latitude, and 2° 50' and 14° 5' east longitude, and are bounded on the north by the French Sudan, on the east by the Kameruns and on the west by Dahomey and French Guinea. The Southern Provinces of Nigeria almost completely adjoin the southern boundary.

The estimate of the populations and areas of the thirteen provinces given below is taken from the Colonial Office Report No. 821 for 1913:—

	Area, sq. miles.	Population.
Sokoto	32,600	1,300,000
Kano	29,500	3,500,000
Bornu	33,600	700,000
Central[5]	23,700	700,000
Zaria	13,320	402,000
Niger[5]	16,770	400,000
Kontagora	27,800	122,000
Ilorin	6,500	200,000

Muri	28,700	700,000
Nassarawa	16,710	600,000
Yola	11,600	300,000
Kabba	8,200	140,000
Bassa	6,700	205,000
	255,700	9,269,000

The total population is thus nearly double that of the estimation of 1907-8. For convenience the Northern Provinces may in places still be referred to in this work by the old title of Northern Nigeria.

As will be seen below there is less variation in the rainfall of the different provinces than is found elsewhere in West Africa. The averages of the following centres for as many years as are available until 1913 are given for comparison:—

	Av. inches.		Av. inches.
Naraguta	50·28	Knepp	40·80
Ilorin	49·75	Yola	38·64
Kontagora	47·77	Kano	33·65
Zaria	46·59	Maifoni	27·85
Baro	46·56	Sokoto	24·86
Lokoja	45·77	Kataguni	19·87
Zungeru	41·67	Geidam	15·14

Of the places mentioned the highest single year's rainfall was reached at Ilorin when 65·18 inches fell, and the lowest at Geidam in 1913 when only 5·76 were recorded. There are localities where the rainfall exceeds the highest given here and others where it is undoubtedly much lower, but no records are available. The highest shade temperatures have been at Dumjeri and Maifoni (North Bornu), where 120° was attained, the lowest being at Kano, where it fell to 39°. In Kano and Zaria rain seldom falls between November 1 and the end of March, but the distribution is more general in the south.

Administration and Political Divisions.—The administration of Northern Nigeria was taken over by the Crown in 1900, having previously been carried on by the Royal Niger Company. Protectorates were gradually assumed, and the country placed upon a secure footing by the suppression of raiding, which had constantly been carried on by the different Emirs, chiefly upon the pagan tribes. The devastation caused by these raids is still visible in the country to the south of Kontagora and elsewhere, and the fear of the raiders kept the inhabitants within or in close proximity to their walled towns, leaving large tracts of fertile country unexploited. The work accomplished by Sir Frederick Lugard, the first High Commissioner, was largely that of pacification and reassurance of the people, and until this had been completed, and facilities for transport provided, it could not be expected that the country could make much progress from a commercial standpoint.

The further opening up of the country by means of roads and railways, and the assessment of land revenue upon lines completely understood and recognised as fair by the natives, was effected by Sir Percy Girouard, who succeeded Sir Frederick Lugard's first administration. Sir Frederick subsequently returned as Governor-General of the amalgamated Nigeria.

Until April 1907 the country was divided into fourteen provinces, one of which, Borgu, was absorbed in Kontagora at that time, making the thirteen mentioned above. By a later reconstruction the provincial limits of the two provinces of Bauchi and Nupe were reformed, and the provinces reconstituted under the names of the Central and Niger Provinces respectively. Groups of provinces were then placed under First-class Residents. Photographs are given of Kano and Zaria (Figs. 32 and 33).

Natural Divisions.—There is less apparent possibility of defining limits to the natural conditions of any part of the country than is found in the countries nearer the coast. There is no afforested zone in Northern Nigeria, although fairly densely wooded tracts occur in several places near the larger rivers. It may be said that grass land studded with well-separated trees is the condition of the country throughout, the trees becoming more stunted towards the northern and desert boundaries. To the north of the 11th degree of latitude, the botanical aspect becomes different; more trees of the Mimosa group, including the gum-bearing Acacias, becoming apparent. Cattle thrive well in this region, where the "tsetse" fly has not yet been observed.

Haussa Land, a term applied to the northern parts of the country, alone among the British West African territories, may be said to have been controlled by an ordered form of government from early times, and to have had a recorded history. Unfortunately these records were destroyed, wherever possible, by the Fulani conquerors, who came from the source of the river Senegal and overran the country at the beginning of the last century, and whose object seemed to be to endeavour to eliminate from the minds of the conquered people all recollection of their previous power. In spite of strenuous efforts in this direction, a few documents have been preserved, and these, combined with traditions, which have not had time to become completely distorted, show that, in spite of severe wars, famines, and other disturbing incidents, the Haussa has maintained his characteristic traits.

The origin of the Haussa race is still a matter of uncertainty, although there is some reason to suppose that it came from the east, and gradually penetrated the Western Sudan from the north. The Haussa language, which is claimed to be more in use than any other native language in West Africa, is said, by Lady Lugard, to be classed with Coptic among the Hamitic languages.[6]

History has established the fact that there were seven divisions or states in Haussa Land, the people of which, although regarded as having come from a common stock, were almost perpetually at war with one another. The mythical account of the formation of these states relates that each had particular duties assigned to it; those of Kano and Rano, to the north of Zaria, being specially industrial. At the beginning of the sixteenth century, when the Songhay kingdom was at the summit of its power, Kano and Gober, among other Haussa towns, were specially referred to by Leo Africanus on account of their cotton trade.[7]

Everywhere along the West Coast the name Haussa is associated with the idea of trade; the itinerant nature of the race inducing individuals to visit the remote parts of the pagan countries, thus creating trade routes in all directions. The Haussa trader of the present day does not necessarily bring goods from his own country for trading, but buys in one market to sell or exchange in another. It is by this means that many European manufactured goods penetrate into localities where no European trader has yet set foot.

The Haussa is also regarded as a good soldier, and is largely enlisted in the native regiments of West Africa under European officers.

The Nupes, Yorubas, Gwaris, Yauris, and others were constantly in contact with the Haussas, and to a small extent the Haussa language is spoken by them. Nupe is regarded as an ancient kingdom, occupying at one time a position of great importance. The Yorubas, who inhabit nearly the whole of the Ilorin Province and the Western Province of Southern Nigeria, trace their origin from the Phœnicians of the tribe of Nimrod, and claim that all the pagan tribes of Haussa Land are descended from them. The Gwaris, apparently, have no records, but are a scattered race living among the rocky hills and caves in the country lying to the south of Zaria.

Bornu was not evidently included in the Songhay kingdom or associated with the Haussa states, the inhabitants belonging to a distinct race with separate traditions. Their history in comparison with that of the Haussas is of recent date. In 1808, after the successful Fulani conquests of Zaria, Zanfara, Kano, Katsena, and Bauchi, Bornu was overrun. Shortly after this a sheikh, from the country extending eastwards from Lake Tchad, believing himself to be inspired to liberate the country, raised a small army, drove out the Fulani forces, and founded the present dynasty of Bornu. Some years later he attempted to expel the Fulanis from the Bauchi Province, but failed, and was compelled to come to terms.

The Haussas as well as the Bornuese are chiefly Mohammedans, but it is only among the higher ranks of the other tribes that a semblance of that religion has been adopted.

The tribes which had migrated from the East brought with them the agricultural knowledge of the Eastern nations. Among the noticeable evidences of this may be mentioned the "shaduf," or dipping beam, used for irrigation in Egypt, which is similarly employed near Kano and Zaria. The absence of ploughs and the non-employment of cattle are, however, difficult to account for, as excellent cattle are common and thrive well in the most populous parts of the country. Tillage of the soil is still done entirely by hand, and, in those parts where the shallowest form exists, manure is extensively used. Among the many crops grown which are common to Oriental countries, as well as Northern Nigeria, are Guinea corn, maize, cotton, groundnuts, millet, benniseed, artichokes, wheat, and rice.

Agriculture shows the greatest development in the Province of Kano, where the population is dense, especially in the vicinity of the town from which the Province takes its name. The concentration of a large population in this locality was doubtless occasioned by the protection thus obtained against local enemies; and, as the realisation of the necessity for this becomes less each year, so will the inhabitants spread out into the richer lands towards the south. At a radius of thirty miles from Kano, it may be said that every available acre of ground is cultivated. It may also be said that nearly all the cultivation is continuous, and has been so for a long period, the renovation of the soil being secured each year by manuring. The mode of cultivation in these localities is for the most part shallow, and in many places the crops grown subsist entirely upon the manure applied. The Director of Agriculture, in the *Bulletin of the Imperial Institute*, vol. xi. (1913), p. 626, refers to the lack of fertility in the soil and to the common practice of cropping without a fallow for a number of years in succession. He also mentions, among other matters of interest, the recent expansion in cultivation of cowpeas and groundnuts; these being respectively third and fourth in order of importance among the cultivated crops.

Implements.—An illustration is given showing the method of using the three important agricultural implements employed by the Haussa cultivator (Fig. 27). The first of these is locally termed "Fatainya," and is a curved-handled hoe with a blade of variable width. It is used for all operations of cultivation with the exception of turning up broad ridges and drilling. The implement shown in the centre is termed "Garma," and is a broad, spade-like hoe, composed of an iron W-shaped frame, with several strips of iron riveted on the face, filling the interval between the arms. In the Zaria Province the iron strips are generally omitted, and the implement is called "Owya." It is used for throwing up large spadefuls of soil in the preparation of the broad ridges which are made for nearly all kinds of crops. The last implement is the "Sangumi," which is a thin rod with a small blade placed near one end and at right angles to it; its use is entirely for making drills for sowing seed.

All the fields for growing ordinary food crops, with the exception of cassava, rice, and sugar-cane, are prepared in ridge formation; the latter appearing to average about 8 in. high from the original surface. The furrows from which the loose soil has been removed increase the apparent height by the extent of their depth, and give the appearance of a good form of tillage having been practised. This is, however, seldom the case, as, except where irrigated crops are being treated, the ground is left untilled beneath the thrown-up soil. To compensate for the shallow state of the cultivation, manure is applied in large quantity, all animal refuse and ashes being carefully preserved, and often conveyed for long distances to the fields by men or donkeys.

The above conditions apparently apply only to the Haussa race, the pagan Gwaris and Bassas resorting to a much deeper form of cultivation and employing no manure. The Nupes and Yorubas do not know the use of manure for any crops except onions and tobacco, for both of which wood ashes are the chief substance applied.

The crops of the country may be roughly divided into rainfall, irrigated, and swamp kinds. The first are sown at the commencement of the wet season, and are greatly affected by the distribution of the rain, but include the most important sources of food. These are Guinea corn, millet, maize, groundnuts, cassava, sweet potatoes, etc. An inadequate or irregular rainy season often causes famine conditions. The irrigated crops are yams, Colocasia, onions, tobacco, peppers, rama-fibre, and wheat, the last being almost confined to the country north of the 11th degree. Cassava and sugar-cane are also frequently irrigated in the drier districts to the north. Irrigation is performed in the northern localities by means of the shaduf. The swamp crops are rice, Colocasia, and sugar-cane. The first is grown upon a flat-dug surface, the second upon high ridges made of swamp mud, and the third on low ridges bordering the rice fields. The villages north of Kano are often entirely built of the stalks of Guinea corn, and Fig. 31 represents a principal hut within such a structure. The fencing of the fields in this locality is generally made of the same material, but in the vicinity of Kano itself, Euphorbia or thorn hedges are more common.

Near Rogo, fences and hedges are usually dispensed with, paths forming the boundaries between fields.

The following table of value of exports shows the progress in the last five years before amalgamation with the Southern Provinces. The subsequent years are given at the end of this chapter.

VALUES OF EXPORTS

	1908	1909	1910	1911	1912
	£	£	£	£	£
Rubber	33,050	40,000	37,900	53,511	[8]
Shea nut products	70,900	93,050	43,150	40,496	51,409
Palm kernels	47,150	41,750	66,100	52,637	64,432
Groundnuts	13,650	16,350	8,150	10,377	18,930
Gum[9]	8,850	6,650	9,750	5,436	1,785
Cotton	1,300	4,400	1,850	945	[8]
Benniseed	2,000	4,000	2,300	2,582	2,972
Fibre	1,382	4,061	—	—	—
Livestock	2,600	1,300	3,750	6,357	9,132
Gutta percha ("Balata")	—	—	2,262	6,695	4,267
Skins and hides[10]	—	—	5,214	37,809	68,832
Ostrich feathers	—	—	2,615	7,225	12,621

RUBBER.—The extent of the export of this commodity from the Northern Provinces was less generally recognised than that from the coast countries, for the reason that the Northern Nigeria's exports are necessarily shipped from Southern Nigerian ports, and have been included in the statistical figures of that country.

Until 1907 no separate statement was furnished indicating the quantity of rubber actually originating from the Northern

Provinces; the whole produce leaving the country by the Southern Nigerian ports made it difficult to ascertain this. The following imperfect records show, however, that the production was of significant extent:

1905.	The value of the rubber exported by two of the leading firms in the Northern Provinces was estimated at £101,207.		
1906.	The amount exported in the second half-year was given as 556,701 lbs., valued at £34,344. The year's exports were said to be 574 tons. Estimating the whole at the same proportionate value as that given for the second half-year we have:		
1906.	1,283,520 lbs.		£79,185
1907.	1,187,588 lbs.		£91,074

The decrease in recent years is accounted for by the fall which occurred in the price of rubber, but is probably partly due to the extermination of the vines by the wasteful process of preparing root rubber.

Sources.—The following are the trees and plants which have been used for extracting rubber:—

1. *Funtumia elastica.*—This is only found in a wild state in Southern Kabba and Bassa Provinces, and is recognised under the Yoruba name of "Ire." Small pieces of fairly well-prepared rubber from this tree are occasionally brought in to Lokoja for sale.

2. *Landolphia sp.* (probably *owariensis*).—A clean "red nigger" rubber is sold, and is probably obtained from this species. It is generally of good quality, but not plentiful. It appears to be

collected as a scrap rubber, and is made up in small irregular balls.

3. *Landolphia sp.*—"Root rubber," termed locally "Attifufu," and called by the trade "Brown cluster" or "Brown medium." It is probable that several species of vines are used for this, which is not necessarily prepared from the root alone, the whole stem being pounded up. This seems to represent the commonest form of Northern Nigerian rubber, the preparation of which was at one time prohibited.

4. *Landolphia florida* or *Thompsonii* (?).—"Paste rubber," called locally "Ebo," is prepared from the latex of these vines by boiling with the admixture of "wood oil," or the resinous exudation of *Daniellia thurifera*, until it reaches the consistency of bird-lime, when it is only capable of being handled in water, in which state it is sold to the merchants, who accumulate it in casks for shipment. It is inferior in quality, and only capable of export for cheap manufactures.

5. *Carpodinus hirsutus.*—"Flake rubber," called "Aribedda," is said to be the product of this vine, which grows commonly in Bassa. It is without resiliency and somewhat resembles the exudations of some of the species of Ficus.

6. *Ficus platyphylla.*—"Red Kano rubber," or "Ballata," known to the Nupe people as "Ogbagba." This is prepared by boiling, without the addition of any foreign matter, and attains the consistency of a hardened paste, similar to the "guttas" made from the latex of the Shea-butter tree (*Butyrospermum Parkii*). It is distinguished in the Kano Province by the name "Danko Gawi," shea gutta being known as "Danko Kadainya."

7. *Ficus trachyphylla.*—This tree is called in Ilorin by the Yoruba name "Oapottoa," and yields a latex which is

discoloured pink by the sap of the tree with which it becomes mixed in tapping. When boiled and allowed to cool, the product is a reddish hardened substance, somewhat resembling gutta-percha in appearance.

8. *Ficus Vogelii.*—Scrap rubber from this tree is said to be collected. In appearance this rubber is often good, but the shreds break up easily.

It will be seen from the above, that several of the so-called rubbers are unlike the valuable kinds in appearance and composition, and as such are, perhaps, incapable of being used in a pure state and for the most important manufactures for which rubber is employed. All kinds, however, seem to be marketable at a price which is remunerative to the exporter, so that the trade has become an extensive one.

Plantations.—It has been urged that Para rubber (*Hevea brasiliensis*) might be grown upon a large scale in the moist and well-watered areas, and Ceara (*Manihot Glaziovii*) and *Funtumia elastica* in the drier districts; but the country is not generally favourably adapted for growing the first and last mentioned. Ceara rubber seems to thrive well in climates similar to that of this country, and the rubber made from it is of the finest quality, but in many tropical countries it has shown great uncertainty in yield of latex, and often unaccountable cessation of flow. This has caused it to be less favourably regarded for plantation work. (Cf. *Bull. Imp. Inst.*, 1913, 1916.)

Many parts of the country are suitable for Ceara cultivation, thriving as it does in localities susceptible to long periods of drought. In the German African Colonies the method of treating the tree seems advantageous, in view of the uncertainty of the yield after maturity is reached. In these places the plants are put out in extensive plots each year, and, after they have reached full growth, all the latex possible of extraction is taken out of them, and the exhausted trees are cut out, permitting the area to become renovated by the self-sown seedlings, which spring up in great profusion. Thus, each year a plot becomes completely renovated, without great expense being incurred. If Ceara planting should be adopted in Northern Nigeria, some such system as this might prove remunerative.

In the Lokoja forest reserve, about a hundred acres of *Funtumia elastica* were planted in 1906, but these have not succeeded as well as was originally expected, owing, probably, to want of moisture. A few Ceara and even Hevea plants, have been grown at Zungeru and Baro, but, as yet, no plantations have been made.

SHEA NUTS.—The shea nut is the seed or kernel contained in the green fruit borne by *Butyrospermum Parkii*, called locally "Kadainya." The fruit, which ripens about May, is of variable size, from that of a pigeon's egg to as large as a hen's egg where only one nut is contained, but is nearly twice the size where two nuts are present in the same fruit. The fleshy rind is not more than one-sixth of an inch in thickness, is sweet to the taste, and contains a white latex, which coagulates into a product called "gutta-shea." The natives in some places seem to regard the fruit as a delicacy, and the roads and paths, in districts where the tree is plentiful, are strewn with the nuts which have been thrown away after the fruit portions have been eaten. The nut is quite smooth, and is readily separated from the fleshy part.

The butter, which is extracted by the natives, is appreciated less than palm oil or groundnut oil for cooking, but is used as a substitute. In Europe the kernels as well as the extracted "butter" are employed, especially on the Continent, for the manufacture of vegetable butter and in candle factories.

In some places the fruits are collected and put in heaps, until the fleshy parts have decomposed and left the nuts clean, after which the kernels are extracted, dried in earthen stoves, and pounded or ground into a fine flour. This is then pounded again, with the addition of a little water, previous to being mixed in hot water to separate the fat. The latter rises to the surface and solidifies on cooling, being melted again for clarification by skimming previous to being poured into moulds made from plantain leaves or maize-cob sheaths. In this form it is sold for export, and is then known as "shea-butter." An illustration is given (Fig. 28) of some Shea nut collectors resting beneath a Shea tree in the Ilorin Province.

SHEA-BUTTER TREE (*BUTYROSPERMUM PARKII*), WITH NUT-COLLECTORS, ILORIN.
FIG. 28

YIELDING GUM TREE (*ACACIA CAFFRA*) AT KONTAGORA.
Fig. 29

LOCUST-BEAN TREE (*PARKIA FILICOIDEA*) AT ILORIN.
FIG. 30

According to results obtained at the Imperial Institute (*Bulletin of the Imperial Institute*, 1908, p. 370; 1912, p. 290), the kernels contain from 40 to 50 per cent. of fat, as well as a small quantity of unsaponifiable matter resembling gutta-shea.

Where the nuts are very plentiful, and transport appears to be easy, the collection is often neglected, and the reason given is that there is some difficulty in removing the fruit from the nut, which makes the occupation unremunerative. But it is noticeable that the fleshy part quickly decomposes, and the clean nuts are frequently seen beneath the trees themselves, although in this situation the advent of heavy rain will often induce germination, and so spoil the kernel. This difficulty is obviated if the fruits are collected and placed under cover, being allowed to decompose without too much moisture.

Throughout the Ilorin and Nupe Provinces the nuts are at present collected for sale to the factories, but in size those grown in the Zaria Province are larger, and are now quite accessible. In this latter locality the double fruit, above referred to, appears to be common. In the tract of country through which the Baro-Kano railway now proceeds, after crossing the Kogin-Serikin-Pawa river, as far Zaria, localities containing very large and prolific trees are frequently met with, but the population is scanty, and collection is scarcely made for export purposes. Trees growing in cultivated areas are generally recognised as the property of the cultivator, forest trees only being common property. Women are the chief collectors of the nuts in the districts whence the supplies at present come, and their inability to penetrate far into the forests has sometimes been urged as a reason for larger quantities not being brought in to the factories. Now that the railway is present, it is probable that regular collectors will commence to exploit the forests for some distance on each side of the line, and that people from the more populous districts will be induced to visit them for the same purpose.

No record is available to show the amount of nuts and butter exported previous to 1905, but it must have been considerable, as the High Commissioner in his annual report for 1905-6 says: "The Shea nut export trade, which formerly constituted the staple of Northern Nigeria, continues to decrease in an unaccountable way, and is now an almost negligible amount." Various reasons are given to account for a partial or gradual decrease, the most important of which is, that the people who used to rely on the collection of sylvan produce for a livelihood, have found a more lucrative employment in growing foodstuffs for the troops and Government staff, or in working upon the Government roads and railways. But, in spite of this, the value of Shea nuts and butter exported in 1907-8 reached a high figure, and placed these products second in order of value among those exported during the year. The export of Shea nuts in the two years following showed a further increase, being 3,922 and 9,085 tons for 1908 and 1909 respectively. There is a growing demand for Shea butter in Europe, and the supply is at present inadequate.

PALM OIL AND KERNELS.—The oil palm (*Elæis guineensis*) is almost absent from a large part of the country, and is rarely seen north of Zungeru, being chiefly confined to the vicinity of the rivers and the forests on the boundaries of Southern Nigeria.

An insignificant amount of palm oil is exported, as the local demand absorbs practically all that is produced, the kernels remaining being alone exported.

Only one variety is recognised in the country, and is that with a thin pericarp and thick-shelled kernel. It is similar to the form termed "Abe-pa" in the Gold Coast. Among the Haussa-speaking races the palm is called "Quaqua," and in the Nupe language "Yi-ku-niche."

Extraction of the oil for local use is generally done by boiling the fresh fruits, and a limpid product is obtained.

GROUNDNUTS.—The groundnut (*Arachis hypogea*), called "Geda" by the Haussas, is seen in two forms in Northern

Nigeria, dependent, probably, on differences in soil and climate in the localities in which they are grown.

The form seen commonly in the vicinity of Bida, from which most of the exported nuts are procured, has a light-brown shell, and is similar to the ordinary Gambian kind. The soil in which this is grown is red, and, to some extent, this colour is imparted to the shell. The nuts growing in the northern districts near Kano, where the soil is sandy and light, resemble the kind which is considered the finest in the French Colonies, and is largely cultivated in Senegal. In this the shell is pale straw-coloured. Large exports have been made from Kano since railway facilities were provided.

Groundnuts are chiefly employed as a terminal crop in the cultivation adopted by the Nupes and Yorubas, but in the Kano and Zaria Provinces, where land is retained for long periods in cultivation and renovated annually by manure, they are often the first crop grown on opening new land, and are seldom planted later.

From an interesting article contributed by Mr. Lamb, the Director of Agriculture (*Imperial Institute Bulletin*, vol. xi. [1913]), entitled "Agriculture in Haussaland," it appears that leguminous crops have recently been introduced more generally in the rotation employed among the Haussa cultivators. The author remarks that the cowpea (*Vigna catjang*) is now almost invariably grown with cereals, and that there is such an increase in groundnut cultivation that this has come into great prominence as an exported crop. This condition has been brought about entirely by the establishment of railway transport—a result which was foretold in the first edition of this work.

All the nuts exported at the present time are in a decorticated form, and the reason given for decortication is that there is a large saving in weight in carriage thereby. It is, nevertheless, generally admitted that in an undecorticated form the nuts are better preserved in transit, and it often happens that the price for undecorticated nuts is higher than for decorticated. It is, however, recognised that if the appearance of the shell is rusty or dirty, it should be removed before shipment, as this condition adversely affects the market value. The demand for undecorticated nuts is for confectionery, and is relatively small as compared with the amount used, chiefly in France, for the expression of oil. The weights of groundnuts exported in 1917 and 1918 were respectively 50,334 and 57,555 tons.

The Kano nuts appear to be of such a clean type that it might be found more advantageous to ship them in an undecorticated state, but this can be ascertained when transport has been facilitated sufficiently to establish a continuous trade with a particular market.

The chief markets for the product were Marseilles and Hamburg, where it was employed for the expression of oil, used principally for admixture with, or as a substitute for, olive oil. Although formerly almost entirely sent to the German port, they now come mostly to England. (Cf. *Bull. Imp. Inst.*, vol. xvi. [1918].)

GUMS.—In the drier regions Acacia trees of several species become plentiful, but many of these do not seem to produce gum.

Some of the gum in the Sudan is said to be derived from *A. arabica*, Willd., which is not uncommon in certain localities, but is almost entirely unproductive in this country.

The tree known in Haussa as "Gawo," identified as *A. Albida*,

Delile, is perhaps the commonest species near Kano, and one which produces a small amount of reddish gum. None, however, is apparently collected from the tree in the district.

The species from which most of the gum is collected in Bornu is said to be identical with that called "Karu" in Kano, of which only immature specimens have as yet been examined. This is probably referable to *A. Verek*, Guill. & Perr., which is the most important source of the Senegal product, and to which Bentham refers *A. Senegal*, Willd.

In Kontagora a good quality of gum is obtained from a tree which has been identified as *A. Caffra*, Willd. This tree does not appear to occur plentifully here, but further investigation is necessary with regard to it in the dry uninhabited regions where it is found. An illustration of this tree is given (Fig. 29).

Another species which has been recorded by Barter from the Niger, and is said by him to yield "a gum like gum-arabic," is *A. mellifera*, Bentham, and may be one of those from which the present exported product is collected.

On examination of the trade specimens, it is noticeable that the quality is inferior to most of the Sudan and Senegal kinds, owing, mainly, to the want of cleaning or sorting previous to sale. It has been suggested that an improvement in the quality might be effected by sorting the gum into different grades, cleaning it, and spreading it in the sun to bleach. The quantity of gum exported in 1908 is given as 789,949 lbs., and that for 1909 as 894,287 lbs.

Investigations carried out recently at the Imperial Institute show that Nigerian gum is little, if at all, inferior to Sudan gum, except that its mucilage is not quite so strong. Gums of the better class are mainly employed in confectionery, and for this purpose the cleaner, lighter-coloured gums of Northern Nigeria are quite suitable. (*Bulletin of the Imperial Institute*, 1908, pp. 29-60; 1910, pp. 352-65; and 1914, pp. 27-31.)

COTTON.—Three distinct forms of cotton are found in cultivation in the Northern Provinces. The best of these is that grown by the natives of the Bassa and Nassarawa Provinces, and possesses lint of rather long staple and a good colour, covering a clean seed. The seed-cotton from these Provinces is brought into Lokoja for sale. This variety seems well suited to the localities mentioned, but, although it has been tried in other parts of the country, it does not seem to thrive so successfully. In making a comparison of the lint for Liverpool market requirements, the standard employed is "Moderately Rough Peruvian," which is a grade of higher price than "Middling American," with which most of the West African cottons are compared.

In Ilorin, a woolly-seeded tall cotton plant is commonly cultivated, and, although yielding a fair quality of lint, it is not equal to that mentioned above. A small proportion of the cotton grown in the Ilorin Province finds its way to the Ogudu Ginnery of the British Cotton Growing Association, on the Niger, but the main crop is carried to various points on the Lagos Government Railway, and is sold for delivery to the Southern Nigerian ginneries of the Association. Small quantities of cotton belonging to this same variety are grown in Nupe, Kabba, and Kontagora, but the low ground of the Niger valley does not appear to be very suitable for cotton-growing.

In Zaria, Kano, and Sokoto Provinces, where the climate is drier, excellent conditions exist for the production of large supplies of cotton, but the population requires to become more distributed into the districts remote from the towns. In the above-mentioned Provinces, cotton has existed from the earliest times, and was long established as an important export to North Africa by caravan. A small-bolled variety with a short stem takes the place of the tall cottons of the Niger valley. The quality of the lint, although fair, is of a shorter staple, and the plant is less prolific.

In addition to the three kinds referred to, all of which are grown as field crops, single plants of a fourth are sometimes seen near villages, especially in the Bassa Province. This is the crimson-flowered tree-cotton identified as *Gossypium arboreum*, var. *sanguineum*, and is nowhere cultivated upon a large scale. The lint is silky and fine, and the seed is covered with green fuzz.

Exotic Cottons.—American and Egyptian seed have been introduced in many localities, especially in the Provinces of the Niger valley. Cotton grown from American Upland seed in Bassa Province has been well reported upon, but the deterioration of the quality of seed reproduced by this kind has proved a serious drawback to establishment. It is generally acknowledged that the indigenous cottons are hardier and more prolific than the introduced varieties, and are better able to withstand the attacks of the local insect pests. It is probable that the climate of the Northern Provinces will be found more suitable for the cultivation of American Upland cottons, as the indigenous plant of that region more nearly approximates the latter type.

Valuation of Cottons.—The following table shows the value of different cottons grown in Northern Nigeria and examined at the Imperial Institute. (See Professor Dunstan's "British Cotton Cultivation," pp. 34-37.)

Locality.	Kind.	Length of Staple.	Value.	Standard value at time of test.
Bassa	American	·9-1·2 in.	7½d.	M.A. 6·39d.
,,	,,	1-1·3 ,,	5½-6d.	,,
,,	,,	1-1·3 ,,	6¼d.	,,
,,	,,	·8-1·2 ,,	6¼d.	,,
,,	,,	1-1·3 ,,	6¼d.	,,
,,	,,	·9-1·4 ,,	6d.	,,
,,	,,	·9-1·3 ,,	6d.	,,
,,	,,	·9-1·2 ,,	6-6¼d.	,,
,,	,,	1·-1·3 ,,	6¼d.	,,
,,	Native	·9-1·3 ,,	6½-7d.	,,
,,	,,	1-1·4 ,,	8½-9d.	M.R.P. 9·1d.
,,	,,	1-1·3 ,,	8d.	,,
,,	,,	·9-1·4 ,,	8¼-8½d.	,,
,,	,,	·8-1·2 ,,	7¾-8d.	,,
,,	,,	1-1·3 ,,	8¼d.	,,
,,	,,	1·2-1·5 ,,	8¼d.	,,
,,	,,	1-1·3 ,,	8d.	,,
,,	,,	·9-1·3 ,,	8½d.	,,
,,	,,	1·1-1·6 ,,	8-8½d.	,,
,,	,,	·9-1·3 ,,	6d.	M.A. 6·39d.
Zaria	Brazilian (?)	·9-1·2 ,,	4d.	,,
,,	Egyptian	·9-1·5 ,,	6d.	F.G.F.B. 10 1/16 d.
Yola	Native	·8-1·2 ,,	4½d.	M.A. 6·39d.

,,	American	·9-1·3 ,,	6¼d.	,,
Munchi	Native	1-1·5 ,,	8d.	M.R.P. 9·1d.
Ilorin	American	·9-1·3 ,,	6¼d.	M.A. 6·39d.

(M.A. indicates the price ruling at the time of valuation for standard "Middling American," M.R.P. that for "Moderately Rough Peruvian," and F.G.F.B. that for "Fully Good Fair Brown Egyptian.")

VILLAGE OF FOGOLA, BUILT OF GUINEA-CORN STALKS.
FIG. 31

OUTSIDE THE EMIR'S PALACE, KANO.
FIG. 32

NEAR THE SOUTHERN GATE, ZARIA.
Fig. 33

All the native cottons in the above table are from the Niger and Benue River Provinces, but it is considered probable that large quantities of the product, which are looked for for export, will be obtained from the Kano and Zaria Provinces, and after the opening of the Baro-Kano Railway, the capitals of these may become important cotton-buying and ginning centres. Figs. 32 and 33 illustrate views of Kano and Zaria.

In all the localities referred to, cotton is generally cultivated as a sole crop, in succession to food crops, and is planted upon shallow ridges from July to September, when the cotton is ready for picking from December to March. Experiments have been made at Baro and Zungeru to raise plants during the dry months by irrigation, but as this causes the fruiting season to occur about the time that the first rain and wind storms commence, the success of this is very uncertain. The necessity for the application of irrigation to this crop is not apparent except as an assistance in lieu of rain when the season of rainfall is late. There is no extreme drought throughout the year, such as is the case in Egypt, where cotton is entirely an irrigated crop.

In the Ilorin district, in the vicinity of Shari, a somewhat extensive area is seen under cotton, and the mode of planting is similar to that applied on a smaller scale near Rabba, Jebba, Bida, and Egga. A piece of land is usually selected for a cotton field upon which Guinea corn and millet crops have been grown continuously for a long period, and which has consequently become rather exhausted. This is often permitted to lie fallow for several years, after which cotton is planted in drills on ridges or mounds in July or August. No manure is applied. Generally about a dozen or more seeds are put in each drill, and in this way it is estimated that about a bushel and a half of seed per acre is required. Picking commences in December, and lasts until February, as much as 500 lbs. of seed-cotton per acre being frequently gathered.

In Kano, cotton is often grown in alternation with cassava, and is a manured crop. Large fields are not seen, as the land is chiefly required for food crops, especially in the vicinity of towns, where the population is dense. General improvements in cultivation, and the introduction of ploughing, would enable a much larger area to be put under cultivation, and would permit of the fertile tracts remote from the towns being employed largely for cotton-growing.

The above account indicates the direction in which efforts should be made to ensure the most fertile tract of Northern Nigeria, where the population is also most industrious and dense, becoming an important cotton-growing locality. It may be safely said that the land, climate, and industrious population are existent and suitable, but the population is congested, leaving large fertile areas of land untouched. Transport difficulties have up to the present prevented cultivation of products useful for export, and the non-employment of cattle for ploughing has restricted cultivation to the growth of crops entirely absorbed by local necessity.

Improvement of Plant.—In addition to these requirements, with regard to cultivation, a rather better class of cotton is necessary in the Northern Provinces. The local variety might perhaps be sufficiently improved under better cultivation and seed selection, but such a process would be gradual and require the undivided attention of an experienced European officer, working in the districts. It has previously been suggested that the introduction of one of the many Upland American kinds might be advantageous; the local variety approaching that class of plant more nearly than do the varieties occurring in the forest regions farther to the south, where the American varieties have been extensively planted with somewhat variable results. One variety only should be introduced, and this should possess cropping and lint records suitable for European requirements. Georgia or Texas quick-maturing kinds are indicated, but not the lowland kinds such as are grown in the Mississippi valley.

The foregoing remarks apply to those regions only where it seems possible that the quality of cotton which is in most general demand in Lancashire can be extensively grown, but are not applicable to the Niger Valley. As will be seen by a reference to the table of valuations, a cotton exists in the Bassa and Nassarawa Provinces which is comparable with a higher standard grade than Middling American, the type to be produced in the north. Efforts should be made to keep this latter variety free from the possibility of admixture with exotic kinds, and it is therefore advisable that improvement in this class should be confined to seed selection. American cottons have already been introduced into Bassa, but the value of the lint is lower than that of the indigenous kind.

With regard to the cotton grown in the Ilorin Province, the common variety is similar to that of the adjoining country to the south, and it is in this direction that the crop of the whole Province will be sent in the future, as it has been arranged to remove the Ogudu ginnery on the Niger, to which the northern Ilorin cotton has hitherto been sent for sale. An illustration is given showing the position of this ginnery upon the southern bank of the Niger (Fig. 34).

The most important insect pests which attack the cotton plant in Northern Nigeria are three species of *Oxycarenus*, or cotton-seed bugs: *Dysdercus superstitiosus*, a cotton-lint stainer, the American cotton boll-worm, *Chloridea obsoleta*, and a species of *Earias*,[11] identical with or allied to the Egyptian cotton boll-worm. The last mentioned has only been recorded as yet from the Bornu Province, but the American boll-worm is found at Lokoja and near the Niger in Nupe. The seed-bugs and stainer are generally distributed. In no direction have these pests assumed large proportions, but where they occur the following remedies are recommended for application. The seed-bugs and stainer can be attracted to traps of seed placed in piles upon the ground between the lines of growing cotton, and the insects then destroyed by petroleum or boiling water. In the case of the boll-worms, trap-crops of maize and Hibiscus are recommended, as well as the destruction of the moths after attraction to light at night. (See Professor Dunstan's "British Cotton Cultivation," pp. 35-6.)

The British Cotton Growing Association commenced work in Northern Nigeria by erecting a steam ginnery at Lokoja, followed by others at Ogudu and Zaria. The natives of the Bassa Province were induced to grow cotton upon a larger scale than before by the favourable market established near them at Lokoja, but, although the cotton brought in was generally of good quality, the supply fell off after the first year or two, and in 1908 it almost ceased. More recently there has been some return to cultivation, but the people are difficult to get into touch with, and have few needs which can be supplied by the traders, so that they have remained somewhat inactive and shy.

The ginnery at Ogudu acted as an inducement to the people of North Ilorin (Shari) to undertake cotton-growing upon an increased scale, and as the inhabitants are chiefly of a more intelligent class (Yorubas and Nupes) than the Bassa people, the cultivation of cotton developed well.

The opening of the Baro-Kano Railway created some activity in cotton growing, and satisfactory quantities were brought in to the northern ginneries. The British Cotton Growing Association will probably succeed well in the northern parts of the country where a large rural population is to be found.

An example of the development of cotton cultivation in West Africa, influenced by and following the opening of a railway, is seen in the Western Province of Southern Nigeria and in Ilorin; along almost the entire route of the line the agricultural population have taken up the cultivation of the plant. This has occurred even in those districts where other natural products were available for utilisation to a remunerative degree. It is therefore probable that the industrious population of the Northern Provinces, who have no such advantages, owing to the absence of oil palms, rubber, etc., would readily adopt cotton-growing upon a commercial scale.

The Baro-Kano Railway passes, however, through an extensive tract of thinly populated country before reaching the localities from which a large supply can be reasonably expected, and this may delay the actual results. It would be inadvisable, in the meantime, to encourage cotton cultivation in those districts which are still remote, unless it were possible to buy the crops in advance of any prospective railway extension.

The following statistical statement has been supplied by the British Cotton Growing Association, showing the production in bales from their ginneries, 1906-1909:

Year.	Lokoja.	Ogudu.	Total.	Weight of Bale.	Approx. lbs.
1906. Sept. 1st, 1905, to Aug. 31st, 1906	903		903	about 200 lbs.	180,600
1907. 16 months. Sept. 1st, 1906, to Dec. 12th, 1907	1,067	815	1,882	200 lbs. each	376,400
		239	239	400 lbs. each	95,600
1908	84	147	231	400 lbs. each	92,400
1909. 8 months. To Aug. 31st, 1909	133	246	379	400 lbs. each	151,600

In 1908 the rainfall was deficient in a large part of the country, and the cotton crop, among others, suffered in consequence. A temporary check to cotton-growing in Ilorin province occurred in 1909 due to the demand for labour for the railway construction, and a subsequent one occasioned by the war; but in spite of this, the increase of cotton in Nigeria is to be attributed largely to developments in the Northern Provinces. Cf. *Bull. Imp. Inst.*, vol. x., p. 480, and vol. xi. pp. 70, 165 and 656.[12]

CAPSICUMS.—An increasing export trade seems to be

becoming established in red peppers and chillies (*Capsicum annuum* and *C. frutescens*), plants which thrive well in West Africa.

In the Ilorin and Nupe Provinces, the plants are usually grown in the vicinity of houses, but in the Kano and Zaria districts they are frequently met with in irrigated fields. From the latter localities an almost unlimited supply could be obtained.

BENNISEED.—The oil seed which is exported under this name is the product of *Sesamum indicum*, Linn., and is identical with that known in India as "til" or "gingelly" seed. Although the specific name seems to imply that the plant is a native of India, there is evidence to show that it may have been introduced into that country from Africa, where several species of the genus occur in a wild state.

The seed is pale or dark brown in colour, and contains a large proportion of oil, for the extraction of which it is exported. In the East, the dark seeds are said to produce the better quality of oil, but this does not appear to be recognised in Northern Nigeria, and the crop grown there is composed of a mixture of the two kinds.

The oil extracted from benniseed is clear yellow and without smell, and is said to be capable of being preserved for a long time without becoming rancid. For this reason it is highly appreciated locally for alimentary purposes, and is said to be used in Europe for making butter substitutes and for mixing with olive oil. The seed cake furnishes a valuable cattle food and good manure.

Although liable to fluctuation in price on the European market, dependent upon the extent of the supply of olive and groundnut oils, the seed is always in demand, and for this reason it is worthy of special attention for cultivation in the fertile and populated tracts of Northern Nigeria.

A fair amount of benniseed is grown in the country, but the use of it is so appreciated locally that only a small quantity is yet shipped, most of this being apparently sent from Bauchi and Kabba, although Kano and Zaria probably produce much more. The value shipped from Nigeria rose from £5,225 in 1915 to £16,523 in 1916.

Benniseed is grown chiefly in separate fields, and is seldom seen in those which have been employed for a long period under Guinea corn or millet. It is a sole crop, and grown but once a year in this country. In India, it may be remarked, the plant is cultivated in both the spring (Rabi) and autumn (Kharif) rotations, and it should be possible to do this in the agricultural parts of Northern Nigeria where irrigation is employed.

KANO LEATHER.—A very large trade exists in the tanned and dyed goat and sheep skins prepared throughout the country, and generally known under the name of Kano leather, or, in Europe, "Morocco Leather." It is said that from early times caravans have annually conveyed numbers of these skins from the Kano markets across the Sahara to the towns in North Africa, whence they were exported to Trieste and other ports of the Mediterranean.

During recent years the caravan trade has almost entirely disappeared, but some quantity of skins now come to Liverpool by way of the coast ports. The value of skins in Kano itself averages about 5½d., but the cost of transport at present has made it almost impracticable to export remuneratively, and a very small trade exists in consequence.

By far the greater number of skins, which are tanned, are

dyed a bright red, yellow, or green colour, which seems to rather depreciate them in the European markets for many uses to which they might otherwise be put, undyed and even untanned skins being in greater demand. (See *Bulletin of the Imperial Institute*, vol. vi. [1908], p. 175; and vol. viii. [1910], p. 402.) It has also been said that the tanning is often insufficiently done, and the skins become blotched in consequence. It is noticeable that Kano leather quickly becomes spotted in the damp coast regions, and for this reason it is probable that no great direct European trade will be established until better methods are introduced and more rapid transport is arranged. There may, however, be a considerable trade done in the untanned skins.

The best class of Kano or Niger leather is valued at a high price for bookbinding.

In the country a fair amount of leather is manufactured for saddlery and horse trappings, pillows, mattress covers, sword scabbards, boots and hats, elaborate designs being often produced by the skilful introduction of pieces of differently coloured leather.

In preparing the leather the skin is stripped off the animal and usually pegged out for drying in the sun, after which it is immersed for two or three days in a liquid made by pounding the pods and seeds of *Acacia arabica* ("Baggarua"), and soaking them in water. The hides are then again pegged out and scraped in order to remove the hair, and when dry the best attain a creamy white colour, others being pale brownish. Palm oil or shea-butter is then rubbed in on the smooth side of the skin, which is worked and rolled until quite soft, after which a polish is obtained by drawing the smooth surface rapidly over a wooden upright blade.

The finest and lightest skins are usually reserved for making into yellow, green, or pale blue leather, and the rest are converted into red, black, dark blue or dark yellow kinds. The red dye is obtained from the stalks of a species of Sorghum,[13] which is grown for this purpose, and to which the Haussas give the name of "Karandeffi" or "Karantudi." The dried stalks are pounded up and placed in a calabash, to which a solution of "potash" is added. A deep crimson liquid results, and in this the skin is steeped until a sufficiency has been absorbed by it to render it permanently deep red in colour. A pale yellow colour is imparted to the skin by an infusion made from the root of a kind of turmeric, which is pounded up for the purpose. A dark yellow is obtained from the root of a tree called by the Yorubas "Agbesi." A black pigment is prepared from a mixture of honey and blacksmith's slag; blue from *Lonchocarpus cyanescens*, one of the indigo producers; green or pale blue-green from brass filings mixed with lime juice, common salt, and other ingredients. More recently green aniline dye has been imported into the country, and has almost superseded the use of brass filings in all the large leather-producing districts.

FIBRES.—Owing to the demand for ropes among the cattle-keepers of the northern districts and the canoemen of the Niger and Benue valleys, it is not surprising to find that the wild fibres are considered insufficient to supply so great a necessity, and that in consequence a selected species is extensively cultivated and prepared for sale in the markets.

"Rama" or "Ramo" is the name which is applied to such a plant in the Haussa- and Yoruba-speaking countries respectively, but although used exclusively for fibre made from plants belonging to the genus Hibiscus, different species are indicated in various districts. The plant to which the name "Rama" is given in Ilorin, Nupe, Kontagora, Kano, and Zaria, is apparently the same as that generally termed "Farin (white) Rama" in Bauchi and Muri, and has been recognised as *Hibiscus lunariifolius*; that called "Rama" in the northern territories of the Gold Coast is said to belong to two species allied to *H. Sabdariffa*, and that grown by the Yoruba people of the western province of Southern Nigeria, and called by them "Ramo," has been identified as *H. guineensis*.

In the present instance only *H. lunariifolius* is referred to, since this is the species cultivated throughout the country.

Although in the other countries the allied plants are cultivated, they are invariably grown upon a small scale, and are only seen in small patches adjoining houses, or cultivated as a mixed crop with peppers, okra, etc.; in Northern Nigeria fairly extensive tracts are planted, and the crop is treated as carefully as the food crops in the vicinity. In Ilorin, Kabba, and Bassa the seeds are sown on ridges in drills a few inches apart, each drill having four to six plants in it. The sowing in this locality is done in the middle of May, and the crop is not irrigated, being dependent upon the rainfall for development. The plants, when they have reached the height of six or more inches, do not appear to be adversely affected by a prolonged continuance of dry weather in the Niger Valley, but this is perhaps accounted for by the humidity of the atmosphere.

The conditions last referred to do not, however, apply to the northern districts, and the importance with which the crop is regarded is seen in the fact that it is worth while to irrigate it. At Fogola the plants are also sown in drills on ridges, but the drills are made at about one foot apart from one another, and ten or more plants are left in each drill. The seed is sown in April and irrigated until the rainy season commences in June.

The stalks are said to be cut after the plant has fruited, and are described as being retted in a manner similar to that employed for Indian jute. The unretted "ribbons" as well as the prepared fibre are offered for sale in the local markets, the former being employed in the rough state for twisting into rope used for fastening roofing poles, etc. The prepared fibre produces an excellent kind of rope, and is in appearance very similar to Bengal jute, although it has slightly less lustre. Specimens of Northern Nigerian rama fibre have been examined from time to time at the Imperial Institute, and have been satisfactorily reported on. As a result the fibre has been actually exported to Europe.

In the *Selected Reports from the Imperial Institute*, Part I., "Fibres" (Colonial Reports—Miscellaneous [Cd. 4588], p. 38), a full account is given of the composition of a specimen of the fibre received from Northern Nigeria. The character is said to be similar to jute, but it is apparently rather harsh, and therefore more suitable for use in rope-making than for spinning. The valuation placed upon it was £12 per ton, with common jute at £11—£12. A specimen of the brown ribbons was also examined and was reported on, the valuation being placed at about £4 per ton, with a remark that it would only be of use for paper manufacture.

During the last three years, since attention was first drawn to the probable value of the fibre as a jute substitute, the natives of Nupe and Muri have been urged to cultivate the plant and prepare the fibre for export. This has been done to a small extent, and the natives of the latter province are said to be willing to produce it at the local price of one penny per pound. At the valuation mentioned above it might scarcely prove remunerative to pay this local price, but it should be taken into consideration that the market price of jute was depressed at the time that the valuation was obtained. It seems that the product may be usefully cultivated, especially in the Niger Valley, where river transport is available, and it is probable that a better price would be quoted if a larger and regular supply could be relied on. The value of the fibre shipped from the country in 1908 is estimated in the Government returns at £1,382, and that for 1909 at £4,049.

Attention should be specially directed to the time of cutting the stalks for retting, and these should be treated before becoming too woody, when a much better product would result.

Experiments with Indian jute, as well as with certain Hibiscus fibres in West Africa, have shown that if the stems are permitted to become woody, the resulting fibre is harsh and coarse.

With regard to the probable production of fibre per acre, there are at present no data, but it may be stated for comparison that a good average yield of jute in India is taken as 2000 lbs. Carefully planted and treated in the same way, it is probable that rama would give as high a return, judging from the growth seen in the country. Jute in India, it should be remembered, is a manured crop, but rama in West Africa is only manured in the northern districts of Northern Nigeria, being cultivated without any special care in the Niger Valley.

WOOD OIL.—Following the order of value shown in the list of exported products, wood oil appears next. This is the oleo-resinous exudation obtained from *Daniellia thurifera*, a tree belonging to the Natural Order *Leguminosæ*, and allied to some of the species from which the West African copals are procured. This tree is commonly found in the dry country, but occurs also in the damp forests, where it frequently attains large dimensions. The wood oil is collected in many parts of West Africa, and is used as a substitute for "balsam of copaiba" in native medicine. The concreted resin formed on the trunks of the trees by the borings of coleopterous larvæ is used for burning as incense.

The native use of wood oil in place of "balsam of copaiba" induced merchants trading upon the Niger to export it, and at one time a fair quantity was sold in England. This export trade has recently diminished to a large extent.

The substance is an oleo-resin, and when free from oil has a similar appearance to copal. Upon examination of the resin, it has been found to be dissimilar in properties from the various freshly exuded resins which enter the market under the name of recent or soft copal. (*Bulletin of the Imperial Institute*, vols. vi. [1908] and xiii. [1915].)

The mode of collecting wood-oil is somewhat destructive, as, in order to procure an excessive flow, a hollow is scooped out in the main trunk and a fire is kindled in the hole thus made. The oil commences to flow rapidly after the fire is extinguished, which it is necessary that it should be before a large quantity of oil has exuded, on account of the inflammability of the latter.

The application of fire to the trees does not appear to kill them, but they are rendered liable to attacks of noxious insects, and are often broken off by winds.

In addition to the local use of the oil for maladies for which balsam of copaiba is generally employed, the rubber makers of Ilorin and Nupe add it to the latex of *Landolphia florida* or *L. Thompsonii* to make paste rubber. The two liquids are boiled together for some time, until the mixture attains a consistency of birdlime. The dried resin is here used for torches, and in the Egyptian Sudan for incense.

KOLA.—Although a large quantity of kola nuts is annually imported from Lagos and the Gold Coast, such a great demand exists that the price of kola in Kano and Zaria is very high. The kola tree is seldom seen in any part of the country except on the west bank of the Kaduna river, where the famous plantations of the Emir of Bida are situated. The kola nuts produced from these plantations are said to be more appreciated than any other, and, in order that the variety might not be grown elsewhere, stringent measures are said to have been enforced by the Emir, and the nuts were always exported to the north, where it was impossible to grow the tree, and where a very remunerative price was obtainable. This particular kind of kola nut is referred to as "Laboji," and is said to be white.

The cultivation of kola could be undertaken in the Kabba and Bassa Provinces, especially in the moist valleys protected from severe winds by high plateaux, such as are commonly found in these localities.

In the export table of 1907 a small quantity of kola is shown, but this probably represents the re-export of produce from the south.

COTTON SEED.—The Lokoja Ginnery has exported a small quantity of cotton seed each year, but the trade is not a lucrative one, and the larger part of the cotton seed which is turned out of the ginnery is valueless for shipment.

FOOD CROPS.—The products which have been referred to above are those which have hitherto been exported from the country, but by far the most important agricultural products are those upon which the population itself subsists, and in relation to which the exported products are merely in the position of a surplus.

Before referring to the products regularly cultivated for food, it is necessary to mention that the seasons, which in the temperate zones are closely associated with a rise and fall in the temperature and its effect upon vegetation, are in West Africa determined to a much greater degree by the advent and cessation of the rainy period. The year is therefore divided into two seasons, roughly described as (1) that in which the conditions are hot and dry, and (2) that in which they are cooler and wet. The vegetation is so directly dependent upon the timely appearance of the rainy season and its normal distribution, that a failure of these conditions, even in a comparatively small degree, may have serious consequences and perhaps produce famine. In no part of British West Africa is a shortage or irregularity of the rainfall so severely felt, nor does it affect such a large number of people, as in the northern districts.

A table is given below showing the distribution of rain in Zaria for five years, and of that in Kano for three years. In each of these it will be seen that the fall in the year 1907 was far below the average, and that during the most important months for the growth of the staple grain crops—July, August, and September—there was a severe shortage of rainfall. The effect of this in Kano was to produce a condition of famine, which lasted for about six weeks. In a congested locality, such as exists in the vicinity of the town of Kano, the difficulty of importing sufficiently large supplies to afford relief at such a period was great, on account of lack of transport. The chief crop in this year, namely Guinea corn, was an almost complete failure in many places, but the millet

Table showing the Rainfall at Zaria for Five Years (1905 to 1909)

Month.	1905.	1906.	1907.	1908.	1909.
January	nil	nil	nil	nil	nil
February	nil	nil	nil	nil	·36
March	nil	nil	nil	·09	nil
April	·76	·85	2·20	1·84	3·56
May	5·90	9·50	3·69	1·91	5·79
June	7·24	5·95	7·05	6·94	6·51
July	7·19	14·49	3·75	7·42	13·11
August	15·04	16·39	4·46	14·36	16·62
September	13·28	9·90	6·33	12·08	6·61
October	1·40	3·93	2·32	·84	1·74
November	nil	·04	nil	nil	nil
December	nil	nil	nil	nil	1·50
Totals	50·81	61·05	29·80	45·48	55·80

(*Pennisetum*) crop, which is an early one, and not dependent on the rainfall after June, had received a normal amount of rain to that time, and was satisfactory; the stored supplies, as well as a second sowing, of this grain to some extent made up for the failure of the other.

The above table has been made out from the meteorological reports obtained at Zaria town, and probably represents a fair average of the rainfall conditions pertaining to the cultivated country in the vicinity.

The more northern district, of which Kano is the centre, is

liable to smaller rainfall conditions than Zaria. A comparison can be made by reference to the table given below.

Table showing the Rainfall at Kano for Four Years (1906 to 1909)

Month.	1906.	1907.	1908.	1909.
January	nil	nil	nil	nil
February	nil	nil	nil	nil
March	nil	nil	·54	·09
April	·01	·10	·23	1·75
May	3·24	1·77	1·16	8·7
June	4·66	5·88	4·12	3·71
July	8·75	3·90	10·24	9·01
August	15·61	9·58	13·92	17·72
September	4·66	3·57	4·63	6·83
October	·87	·01	·02	·77
November	nil	nil	nil	nil
December	nil	nil	nil	·45
Totals	37·80	24·81	34·86	49·03

The remarks made above serve to emphasise two points in connection with the densely populated districts of the north, the first being the necessity of cultivating larger areas to permit of surplus supplies being stored, and the second the requirement of quick transport to enable supplies to be brought in from the Niger valley in cases of urgent need. The first of these also indicates the necessity for the improvement of agricultural methods by the introduction of ploughing, the extension of irrigation and dry-season crops, and the better distribution of the population. The second—the supply of quick transport—is becoming rapidly established, by means of the railway and improved roads.

The extension of irrigated crops can only be made in the vicinity of the larger rivers, or where good wells exist, and it may be found more expedient, therefore, that the inhabitants of the Niger, Benue, Kaduna, Gongola, and Gurara valleys should be urged to cultivate rice and maize under these conditions. The use of the land for two crops in each year would be made possible by the introduction of a leguminous crop as an intermediate, being sown later but in the same field with the irrigated crop, and being permitted to ripen, after the grain has been harvested, upon the stubble. A leguminous grain suitable for human food would be necessary in the river valleys where cattle are scarce, but a cattle food could be grown in the north where cattle are common, and where milk forms an important article of human consumption.

GUINEA CORN (*Sorghum vulgare*)—"Dawa" (Haussa), otherwise known as the Great or Indian Millet "Juar" (Hindustani), "Dhura" (Egyptian)—forms the most important food-grain of the inhabitants of the ultra-forest region of West Africa.

A large number of different varieties are recognised in Northern Nigeria, and are distinguished in the manner stated below. Most of these have a grain which is commonly used for human food, but at least two varieties are grown for other purposes.

The following list states the characters by which the various kinds can be determined from the appearance of the seed and form of the stem.

1. "Asidinono."—Seed with white shell and black adherent envelope.

2. "Farafara."—Seed with white shell and red adherent envelope.

3. "Boganderi."—Seed with straw-coloured shell and red adherent envelope.

4. "Janari."—Seed with pink shell and red adherent envelope.

5. "Kaura-ferin-sosia."—Seed with straw-coloured shell and straw-coloured adherent envelope.

6. "Bokin-sosia."—Seed with straw-coloured shell and black adherent envelope.

7. "Makafo-dewayo."—Seed with straw-coloured shell and pointed straw-coloured adherent envelope, which scarcely opens.

8. "Asidigero."—Small pink-shelled seed with red adherent envelope.

9. "Mazgua."—Very large whitish seed with a straw-coloured envelope.

10. "Karandeffi."—Seed with red shell and red adherent envelope. Never used for food, but employed in native medicine, as well as for the production of the red dye used for leather (*Bull. Imp. Inst.*, vol. vi. [1908]).

11. "Takanda" or "Karantalaka."—The seed has not been examined, but the stem contains a large quantity of saccharine juice, and the plant is grown entirely as a cattle food. Probably identical with *S. saccharum*.

The first four kinds are regularly employed as food, and are found growing as a mixed crop; although the white grains are more appreciated and frequently predominate. Nos. 5 and 6 are not considered so good for human food, but are largely employed for feeding cattle and horses, for which latter purpose they are greatly in demand. No. 7 is used for the same purpose as the last, but is a rarity and of no special value. These seven kinds are grown as six-months' crops, and are harvested in October when the rains cease. No. 8 is a three-months' cropping kind, which in this particular resembles "Gero" (*Pennisetum typhoideum*), as its native name indicates. The grain is much smaller than the others, and it is said to be cultivated to some extent in the Sokoto Province. No. 9 is a variety which is said to be cultivated in Bornu in the fertile depressions which retain moisture for long periods, or by means of irrigation from the rivers. (See *Bulletin of the Imperial Institute*, vol. iv. [1906], p. 226.)

Guinea corn is permitted to occupy the land for a number of years successively, being often grown with "bulrush millet" (*Pennisetum typhoideum*). In this case the millet occupies the furrow whilst the Guinea corn is on the ridge, and this is reversed when the soil from the ridge has been hoed into the furrow and the previous ridge becomes the furrow. In many parts of the northern districts it is customary to permit the Guinea corn root-stocks to remain in the ground for two or three years, and to fill in the vacancies only with new seed when the old plants die. By this system it is found that the crops are better assured, as the old root-stocks withstand a prolonged drought better than new plants. This custom, if persisted in, would be a direct hindrance to the introduction of ploughing.

Manure is applied regularly to this crop in the northern districts, but never in the Niger valley. The method of applying manure varies according to the condition of the crop. Where entirely new plants are to be grown, a shallow bed is made upon the top of the ridge or in the furrow, and the goat, sheep, and cow manure mixed with ashes, and accumulated carefully in the villages, is spread thinly upon the bed before the seed is sown. In other places, where old root-stocks occur, handfuls of manure are applied to the growing plants in May. This is sometimes adopted where young plants only are growing. Manure is so necessary for the system of cultivation adopted in the Kano and Zaria Provinces that every scrap of material which is of manurial value is carefully preserved, being carried to the fields by men and donkeys.

The heads are cut when ripe and tied in bundles to dry, after which the grain is readily beaten out in wooden mortars or with sticks. The flour made from the grain is ground between stones, and is frequently eaten in the form of a thin porridge. Two varieties of Nigerian Guinea corn have been examined at the Imperial Institute and shown to be superior to Indian Guinea corn, though not quite so good as the Syrian grain (*Bulletin of the Imperial Institute*, vol. vii. [1909], p. 148.)

Smut-blights, *Ustilago Reiliana* and *Tolyposporium sp.* (called in Haussa "domana"), attack the heads, and a *Capnodium sp.* (called "derba"), the honeydew produced on the leaves by *Aphis sorghi* (cf. *Bull. Imp. Inst.*, vol. xi. [1913]).

At certain stages, green Guinea corn is poisonous to cattle, and for this reason goats, sheep, and cows are muzzled in the Kano and Zaria Provinces. Local knowledge of this fact confirms what has been observed elsewhere with regard to this species, and is explained by investigations conducted at the Imperial Institute. (*Bulletin of the Imperial Institute*, vol. i. [1903], and vol. viii. [1910].)

BULRUSH MILLET.—This plant, which is supposed to be of African origin and is usually called millet in West Africa, belongs to that group of grasses of which the seeding head is in a compact form and in appearance resembles the head of a bulrush, from which the common name applied to it has been derived. The botanical name is *Pennisetum typhoideum*, and the plant is known in the country as "Gero" or "Giro" (Haussa), and in India as "Bajra." At least two varieties, a smooth and an awned form, are grown as three-months' crops, and are sown either alone or as described before with Guinea corn. It is usual to plant millet seed before the Guinea corn, generally about the middle of April, or as soon as the first showers are experienced. The crop is then ready for picking in June and July. If the rainfall by this time has been deficient to such an extent that the Guinea-corn crop promises to prove a failure, a second crop of millet is often put in, and, as very much less rain is required for this crop than is necessary for Guinea corn, the severe effects of a short rainfall are minimised. The grain yielded by *Pennisetum typhoideum* would be classed commercially as a millet, and a sample from Nigeria examined at the Imperial Institute was valued at 22*s*. per quarter of 480 lb. (July 1908).

In addition to the two varieties mentioned which are employed as three-months' crops, there is another kind with a smooth greyish-white large grain which is called "Maiwa" or "Dauro," and is cultivated in the same manner as Guinea corn; occupying the land for from five to six months. The pagan Gwaris to the south of Zaria grow this in large quantities, but it is uncommon north of Zaria.

These grains are easily stored, and keep in good condition for a long time. Flour is made from the grain by grinding, and both the grain and leaves are used for cattle food.

From the malted grain of millet, and sometimes of Guinea corn, an intoxicating beverage is made which is known as "Gir" (Haussa).

A fine grass seed called "Acha" (*Digitaria ternata*) is grown in the fields with millet, and attains a height of about two and a half feet. It is used for making a sort of porridge. "Tomba" (*Eleusine coracana?*) and "Iboru" are grown in a similar manner. The composition, nutritive value and commercial value of several of these food grains are fully dealt with in the *Bulletin of the Imperial Institute*, vol. vii. [1909], p. 148.

BRITISH COTTON GROWING ASSOCIATION GINNERY, OGUDU, ILORIN.
Fig. 34

GWARI TOWN, OPPOSITE MINNA, SOUTH OF ZARIA.
Fig. 35

COW FULANI WOMAN SELLING MILK AT GWARI.
Fig. 36

MAIZE.—"Mussara" (Haussa) is the name applied to this plant (*Zea mays*). The crop is more common in the Niger valley among the Nupe and Yoruba people than in the higher plateaux of Zaria and Kano. It is probable that maize requires a larger rainfall than the grain crops which have been mentioned above—which may account for the infrequency of its cultivation in the dry country.

Among the Gwari pagans, inhabiting the country in the vicinity of Minna, and the Nupe people to the south, fairly large quantities of maize are grown and seem to represent the chief food crop. The sowers drop only one seed, or at most two, into the drills, where they would put five or six Guinea-corn seeds. The only variety grown commonly has a bright yellow grain and is apparently a three-months' crop; being sown at the commencement and in the middle of the rains, thus giving two crops in the year in some localities. An illustration is given at Fig. 35 showing a view of the Gwari town at Minna.

WHEAT.—The cultivation of wheat is confined to the drier parts of Northern Nigeria, where it is grown as a rainfall as well as an irrigated crop.

In Zaria it is frequently sown in October, and occupies land which may have been under rice cultivation just previously. Goat manure is especially applied to wheat, and irrigation is carried out from wells or by the employment of shadufs on the banks of streams. This crop is harvested in January.

In Kano, wheat is more generally grown as a rainfall-crop in similar situations, and is, in this case, sown in May, being harvested in September.

The variety seems to be constant throughout the country, and appears to have been established from very early times. The grain is similar in appearance to the wheat seen in the Nile valley, and may be *Triticum compositum* (Egyptian wheat). Specimens from Kano and Zaria have been examined at the Imperial Institute, and the analyses made show about 11 per cent. of gluten including 5 to 6 per cent. of gliadin, and the commercial experts consulted were of opinion that an unlimited quantity of this type of wheat would be readily saleable on the European market (*Bulletin of the Imperial Institute*, vol. viii. [1910], p. 118.) The Kano wheat in particular gave excellent results in milling and baking trials.

As a food, wheat is regarded with great favour in the country, and is bought up chiefly by the wealthy classes for making a brown flour. It makes an excellent bread, and is in demand among the European residents for mixing with European tinned flour for breadmaking.

In order to separate the grain from the ear, the dried corn is threshed by the village women; thin sticks being used for the purpose. The chaff is then winnowed in the wind. The Haussa name is "Alkama."

In addition to Zaria and Kano districts, the grain is said to be plentiful and cheap in Sokoto and Bornu, but does not appear to be grown south of the 11th degree.

RICE.—The cultivation of rice extends over a much larger portion of the country than wheat. It is said to be especially plentiful in the low-lying districts to the south of Sokoto, where large tracts of swampy country exist, which are annually planted with the crop. On the banks of the Kaduna river, near Dakman and Dagomba, as well as in the valley of the Baku river in the Nupe country, irrigated rice fields are common, and the product from the Nupe Province is much appreciated by the inhabitants of the middle Niger. The local name for rice is "Shinkafa."

Near Zaria and Kano comparatively little rice is cultivated, and where seen is generally found in swampy places where other food grains are not capable of being utilised. Rice in these localities is one of the few unmanured crops, and is planted at the commencement of the rainy season. The harvesting is done about November or December, and the paddy or husk-rice is cleaned by soaking the grain in hot water, drying in the sun and then pounding in a wooden mortar. The chaff is winnowed, and a fairly clean rice with a slight reddish tint remains. All the rice appears to be of the same type, and is held in high estimation for its nutritious quality. The imported white rices, which occasionally enter the country, are regarded with less favour than the local kind.

It is possible to develop the cultivation of the crop in the valleys of all the large rivers, and it seems probable that, with improved methods of irrigation, two crops might be grown annually.

A sample of rice from Ilorin examined at the Imperial Institute proved to be about equal in quality to average Bengal rice (*Bulletin of the Imperial Institute*, vol. vii. [1909], p. 149), but it is improbable that it would at present prove remunerative to export this rice to Europe. A good market might, however, be found for it at the coast ports of Southern Nigeria, where imported rice is in demand. It might be necessary, in order to compete with the present trade, to grow and prepare a cleaner (less red) variety, which would resemble more nearly the imported kinds, and to this end the acclimatised American rice of Sierra Leone might be tried (cf. *Bull. Imp. Inst.*, vol. xv. [1917]).

SUGAR-CANE.—The cultivation of sugar-cane (*Saccharum officinale*) is confined to small patches or strips of land on the edges of rice fields, where it may be said to be under irrigation. The Haussa name is "Reke." The preparation of sugar does not appear to be known in the country, and the sole use to which the plant is put, seems to be the consumption of the green stalks by the inhabitants and their cattle. The variety seen in Kano district appears to have a reddish stalk, and cane is said to be a feature in the Maigana district.

LEGUMINOUS PLANTS.—Several kinds of small beans are grown, of which the most valuable appears to be that known as "Wanki." This is a white-skinned kind, similar to, but about half the size of, the white haricot of Europe. The cultivation of these beans is somewhat irregular; a few being occasionally sown among the millet and Guinea-corn crops. They are apparently never grown as a sole crop. A similar bean of a brown colour is common in the Bassa Province, but the white bean is generally distributed throughout the whole country.

The "Bambarra groundnut" (*Voandzeia subterranea*) is grown in a similar manner to the common groundnut (*Arachis hypogea*) which has been referred to among the exported products. The cultivation is similar, and the plant is seen occupying elevated ridges. The Haussa name is "Paruru."

An unidentified bean, which is called "Girigiri," has been described as being grown by the pagan Gwari tribes to the south of Zaria, but apart from the fact that it is much larger than the "Wanki" bean, nothing seems to be known about it.

Indian dhall (*Cajanus indicus*), frequently termed the pigeon pea, has been introduced into many parts of the country, with the object of inducing the native to grow a leguminous crop, which would serve the dual purpose of providing a palatable food as well as being beneficial to the soil, but in only a few localities do the natives appear to make use of the peas for food. It has been recommended to grow the plant upon land which has become somewhat exhausted by the repeated growth of grain crops, and to permit the peas to remain upon such land for two or three seasons, during which time they will yield successive crops. The beneficial action which such a plant exerts by nitrifying the soil, and the manurial value of the leaves, which are shed in thick profusion, are important reasons for its introduction, but the value will not be fully appreciated until it has been adopted generally as a food.

SOYA BEAN.—The Manchurian or soya bean (*Glycine hispida* or *soja*), which has the additional merit of yielding about 15 per cent. of a valuable oil, and which is highly appreciated as another kind of dhall in India, is being experimented with in various parts of British West Africa (see *Bulletin of the Imperial Institute*, vol. viii. [1910], p. 40).

The recent expansion in the cultivation of leguminous crops is a promising step.

CASSAVA.—Among the Haussas as well as the Yorubas and Nupes, the cultivation of cassava (*Manihot utilissima*) is extensively carried on. In Haussa cultivation it is an unmanured plant, and is usually grown in separate fields surrounded by mud walls, thorn hedges, or Guinea-corn matting. The ground from which a crop of cassava has been harvested is rarely used for Guinea corn; the succeeding crop being usually cotton, with the application of manure. In the Nupe country, near Bida, cassava is frequently employed as a shade crop for onions; in this case being planted around the onion beds and obtaining the benefit of the high state of cultivation, manuring and irrigation which is applied to that crop. Cassava grown under these conditions is planted twenty days later than the onions, and is pulled up a month later.

The pagan tribes of Zaria, and the other provinces where they are in greater numbers, do not seem to plant cassava. The Haussa name given to the plant is "Rogo."

YAMS (*Dioscorea sativa*, etc.).—These climbers are commonly grown in the moist valley of the Niger and in the Yoruba country of Ilorin, but are rare and only an irrigated crop in the more northern countries. Where they are seen, they are planted from root eyes upon high mounds with ditches dammed to retain the water between them, and, until the plant has grown up as a trailer upon the ground, some feet in length, no supports are put in. At this time, however, the straw covers, which it is customary to place on the apex of the yam mounds, are removed and an elaborate system of stakes, to the top of each of which strings are tied and conducted to the ground near the growing plant, are put in, and the plants to the number of four or more are trained to grow towards the top of each stake.

The large white yam is chiefly grown, and is called in Haussa "Doya." Yams attain large dimensions in the damp localities, but are small in the drier places.

Colocasia antiquorum, called by the Haussas "Kamu," is usually referred to as the koko yam and is rarely grown. A few may be seen in the wet localities and near Zaria, where they are planted in swamps upon high mounds or ridges.

SWEET POTATOES.—This crop is grown everywhere, and is nearly always unmanured. It is said that it forms the occupant of the land upon which Guinea corn and millet are repeatedly grown in some parts of the Kano district in the second and eighth year—*i.e.* twice in a period of eight years. In the year of plantation, the ridges are said to be heightened. Near Bida very high beds are made for it, resembling flat-topped mounds, with an area of sixteen or more square feet. The Haussas apply the name "Dankali" to the root, which is usually of the small white variety.

Artichokes and small Root Crops.—The Jerusalem artichoke (*Helianthus tuberosus*) called "Gwaza," as well as "Rizga" (*Plectranthus sp.*) and "Tumuku" (probably *Plectranthus sp.*) are cultivated by the people living to the south of Zaria Town.

"Gwaza" seems to be less planted than "Rizga," the latter being carefully grown upon selected ground which has been previously hoed and levelled, the surface being covered over with branches of *Bauhinia reticulata* and other forest plants until the stems of the crop have reached a height of one foot or more. Single stems spring from the root eyes which are planted. "Tumuku" resembles "Gwaza" in appearance, but comes up in clusters of stems and is planted upon mounds.

All the above roots are used in the manner in which the potato is employed in Europe; cassava alone being pounded to make a kind of dough ball, in addition to being eaten in chopped up and boiled form.

Onions.—Two kinds of onions are cultivated throughout the country: *Allium cepa*, the large onion which is seen to perfection in the Kano markets, and *Allium ascalonicum* which is usually termed the shallot, and is cultivated to a larger extent in the localities where manure is scarce.

The variety of large onion grown in Kano is pink upon the outside, and for this reason, according to inquiries conducted by the Imperial Institute, is said to be quite unsuitable for the English market; the white Egyptian onion being preferred.

Cultivation.—The cultivation of onions is, perhaps, more carefully carried out than that of any other crop, and may be described from that seen at Lemu in Nupe. The seed is sown closely in beds of soil which have previously been enriched with manure, and the surface is covered with straw until the young plants are a few inches in height. Transplanting into new beds, which are strewn with cow and goat manure, is the next operation, the plants being put in at about 4-6 inches apart. The whole cultivation is done during the dry season, and the beds are irrigated by means of channels supplied with water raised from streams or wells, in the north by shadufs, or in the Nupe country by people conveying the water in calabashes.

The market price varies greatly in different districts, and is immediately influenced by any reduced supply. There is said to be a very good demand for the large onions in the Southern Nigerian markets, and there should be no difficulty in getting them to Lagos, as they have been brought from Kano to London in good condition.

Minor Crops.—Okra (*Hibiscus esculentus*), "Kubiewa," a species of Solanum resembling a small tomato called "Yalo," the sorrel Hibiscus (*H. Sabdariffa*) called "Yakwa," a pumpkin called "Kubiwa," and the aubergine (*Solanum melongena*), are grown upon a small scale, and chiefly in the vicinity of houses.

OTHER FIELD CROPS. Dye Plants.—Indigo is the chief dye used in the country, and is prepared in the northern provinces from a species of Indigofera, which has not been accurately determined.

In Ilorin and Kabba the plant used is *Lonchocarpus cyanescens*, and the wild trees of this species may be seen preserved in the cultivated fields.

Camwood, a name applied to the red wood obtained from several species of *Pterocarpus* and from *Baphia nitida*, in different parts of West Africa, is obtained chiefly from *P. erinaceus* in Northern Nigeria, and is used by the natives for staining the skin. It is preserved in the fields cleared for grain cultivation.

Henna is obtained from *Lawsonia inermis*, which is regularly planted as a sole crop in the northern provinces and Kontagora. The use of it is generally to replace camwood as a red dye where that tree is scarce.

Tobacco.—The cultivation of tobacco (*Nicotiana tabacum*) is carried on in almost every part of the country, but for native use is generally made into snuff or into ropes, plaits, and targets, for sale in those places where it is smoked. (Cf. *Bull. Imp. Inst.*, vol. xv. [1917], p. 32.)

The crop is usually grown in the river valleys, and is irrigated carefully. Manure in the form of house sweepings, ashes, and cattle-shed refuse is always applied, and the crop consists of leaves of all sizes and ages stripped from the plant at the same time.

The preparation of the tobacco usually consists in drying the leaves spread upon mats or upon sand in the sun. When flaccid they are twisted into ropes or plaits in the form in which they are afterwards sold, or they are completely dried and pounded up. In Ilorin an attempt has been made to prepare the leaves tied up in flat bundles, and this method has more recently been tried at the Baro prison farm, but the previous curing has generally proved inefficient and requires more attention. It is unlikely that tobacco fit for export will be produced except under expert guidance.

MISCELLANEOUS. Beeswax.—Bees are kept in many of the large villages, and are seen in hives placed in trees near the large towns in Kano and Zaria especially. Honey is employed in the country as a substitute for sugar. The wax is not greatly valued, and is frequently thrown away, although it seems to be of fair quality.

Locust Bean.—The tree which furnishes the well-known locust bean (*Parkia filicoidea*) is called "Dorowa" by the Haussas. The beans, which are produced in clusters, contain a sweet-tasting yellow flour-like substance, which is used for making a beverage. In this flour-like substance the flattened seeds are placed, and these are greatly appreciated for making into cakes, in the process of which they are boiled and apparently decomposed. The empty pods of the bean are boiled and used for making a strong cement used in flooring, etc. The pods have been examined at the Imperial Institute, and appear to be unsuitable for export as a feeding-stuff owing to their fibrous nature (see Report by Professor Dunstan on "Cotton, Gum, and Other Economic Products from Northern Nigeria" (Cd. 2778 [1905]), p. 21). Fig. 30 shows a locust bean tree in Ilorin.

Date Palms (*Phœnix dactylifera*) and the fruit of the Run palm (*Borassus flabellifer*), "Giginia" (Haussa), are used for food and are sometimes sold in the markets towards the south, being commonly seen in Kano.

CATTLE.—Large numbers of cattle are moved about through the country north of the 11th degree, where the tsetse fly does not appear to occur. The "Cow Fulani" is the race whose work is confined to the care of cattle and the sale of milk and butter. These people have no fixed abode, but move with the cattle to localities suitable to the season. An illustration is given of a Cow Fulani woman selling milk at Gwari, a town south of Zaria (Fig. 36). The cattle are large and humped similar to the Indian Zebu type, although in some places the straight-backed kind, which are common in the south, are seen.

SILK.—Four kinds of silkworm are collected for the spinning of yarn used in the embroidery on the Haussa gowns. The best of these is that which feeds upon the Tamarind tree, "Tsamia," and is termed "Tsamian tsamia." The silk cocoons are collected in Bauchi Province and are boiled in water with wood ashes, and subsequently washed. The silk becomes nearly white, and is carded and spun into yarn in the same manner as cotton. The species of insect which produces this silk has not yet been identified, but is almost certainly referable to the genus *Anaphe* (cf. p. 117).

A second quality of silk is that called "Tsamian doka," and is obtained from the cocoon masses produced by the larvæ of *Anaphe Moloneyi*, which are found in the same locality, feeding upon the "Bokin doka" tree, which has been determined to be a species of *Macrolobium*. Several hundred worms congregate together and form a solid mass of pale brown tubular cocoons upon the bark of the tree, covering the outer surface with a whitish envelope of silk. This silk is treated in the same manner as the other, but, after boiling and washing, does not become white. Two other species, which are used for the same purpose, are called "Tsamian fakali" and "Tsamian bauri," and feed on another species of *Macrolobium* and a *Ficus* respectively. They produce inferior kinds of silk.

Much interest is attached to these Anaphe silks, which, in recent years, have been developed in the German Colonies of East Africa, especially, on a commercial scale. It is reported that, just previous to the declaration of war, German agents in British West Africa made endeavours to obtain as much of the wild silk as possible from Nigeria. Plantations of a species of *Bridelia*, the common food plant of *Anaphe infracta*, were made in the late German Colonies, and special machinery was in use there for the production of a commercial silk.

The following figures give the values of the chief exported products from Nigeria as a whole, from 1913 to 1919:—

	1913	1914	1915	1916
	£	£	£	£
Palm kernels	3,109,818	2,541,150	1,692,712	1,739,706
Palm oil	1,854,384	1,571,691	1,462,162	1,402,799
Cocoa	157,480	171,751	313,946	393,101
Cotton lint	159,223	150,791	56,351	243,949
Mahogany and timber	106,050	86,522	54,559	49,361
Groundnuts	174,716	179,219	72,177	473,653
Hides and skins	197,214	505,785	302,420	538,917
Shea products	74,471	52,843	69,823	32,529
Rubber	—	38,854	38,113	34,192
Benniseed	—	—	5,225	16,523

Continued:	1917	1918	1919
	£	£	£
Palm kernels	2,581,702	3,226,306	4,947,995
Palm oil	1,882,997	2,610,448	4,245,893
Cocoa	499,004	235,870	1,067,675
Cotton lint	234,338	97,399	484,744
Mahogany and timber	21,282	68,480	116,820
Groundnuts	710,308	920,137	698,702
Hides and skins	198,332	293,019	1,262,142
Shea products	40,189	4,884	37,222
Rubber	32,350	19,667	43,903
Benniseed	2,876	696	53,541

FOOTNOTES:

[1] Hinchley Hart, in *Cacao*, 1892, pp. 48-52, discusses the three varieties mentioned here, and shows that intermediate forms exist which connect all three. The *Forastero* class includes all the cocoas which have thick skins and large pods with rather flat beans.

[2] *S. singularis*, a nearly allied insect, is common in certain localities and does similar damage.

[3] Cf. *Bull. Ent. Res.*, vol. i. (1911), p. 83; *Bull. Imp. Inst.*, vol. viii. (1910), p. 150; vol. xiv. (1916), p. 174; vol. xviii. (1920), p. 319.

[4] This has since been identified with *Gelechia gossypiella*, Sanders, an insect which subsequently effected such enormous damage in Egypt.

[5] These names are substituted for Bauchi and Nupe in the old system.

[6] Lady Lugard, *A Tropical Dependency*, 1905, p. 236 *et seq*.

[7] *Ibid.*, p. 209.

[8] Included in Southern Nigeria exports.

[9] Including copal resin.

[10] Including dressed skins.

[11] Identical with what is termed *E. biplaga* at Ibadan, but probably a local form of *E. insulana*.

[12]For the most recent information respecting cotton cultivation here and elsewhere in West Africa, Professor Dunstan's Reports to the Brussels Congress of Tropical Agriculture (1910) should be consulted.

[13]Since named *S. guineensis* var. *robustum*, Stapf.

www.ingramcontent.com/pod-product-compliance
Lightning Source LLC
Chambersburg PA
CBHW071706160426
43195CB00012B/1591